HEALING
LIFE'S
SORE
SPOTS

HEALING LIFE'S SORE SPOTS

FRANK A. KOSTYU

HAWTHORN BOOKS, INC.
W. Clement Stone, Publisher
NEW YORK

Dedicated to
Joel
Paul
Kathryn

Table of

Contents

Preface

As we consider the metaphorical "sore spots" in our lives, one thing stands out. We are all subject to these bruises of the spirit, regardless of age, financial status, background, or education. Upon further thought, we come to the conclusion that in order to be healed, we must grow in understanding and belief. We must make the effort.

Since we are all individuals, our sore spots differ in intensity and importance. No book, therefore, would apply equally to all people. Through the various chapters, which zero in on common problems, I attempt to point out distinctive aspects of these sore spots and by discussion and examples lead you, the reader, to a point where you feel the healing power in your own life and can apply personally the principles brought out.

This book is written as a guide by which you can obtain suggestions on how to treat your own problems. It culminates in a chapter on the use of prayer as an ever-present source of strength, a medicine you can use to help heal your own sore spots.

In no sense is this a technical book. Rather it is one written out of experience, both personal and pastoral, gained in dealing with real situations. Over the years, these suggestions have helped others. They can help you.

HEALING
LIFE'S
SORE
SPOTS

LONELINESS

1

Solitary and Light Blue

Loneliness is many things to many people, universal, many-faceted. Persons of all ages, races, creeds, and personalities feel it in varying forms and in varying degrees. An emotion is not necessarily a physical condition; it deals with the mind and the heart. Whether of long or short duration, loneliness has the power to create changes or to devastate a personality; it can be both creative and destructive. It can be a sore spot in the life of one who has not learned to use this solitariness to his advantage.

The following lines by my son, Paul Kostyu, bring out one aspect of loneliness:

> Yes, I will be alone,
> Alone, by myself.
> I will exist in a place
>
> Where no one will want to see me,
> Where no one will want to hear me,
> Where no one will want to touch me.

3

I will be alone with my thoughts;
   My mind will exist in a state of confusion,
Confused with dreams and ideals
   Yet lacking in reality.
I know not where this place is.

I will be apart from the living and not living
But I will be there, and
   I will be alone.

Some individuals welcome loneliness as a time to know themselves, while others fear it and will go to great lengths to avoid it. Still others simply accept loneliness as it comes, knowing that through its very existence they touch a universal condition of man.

We All Know Loneliness

Nostalgia is the in thing right now. Recall, therefore, some moments of your childhood. Do you remember a dark, cold, windy night, when you awoke with a start and suddenly realized how alone you were?

No reassuring hand reached out toward yours. Or perhaps you were left out of a ball game or were not invited to a party. Even physical abuse or punishment can be preferable to being "sent to Coventry." The West Point cadet who endured many months of such ostracism could attest to the hurt involved in such loneliness.

People in high places, supposedly surrounded by exciting and important personages, can be lonely. In whom can they confide? Can they have truly close relationships with others, untouched by prestige or favor seekers? Being alone is a part of the lives of presidents, kings, military leaders, religious leaders, writers, artists, and inventors. Many have found a measure of solitude to be essential in their lives.

In the comic strip "Ziggy," Tom Wilson, its creator, has Ziggy standing on a hill looking at a flower. Ziggy says, "Little flower, you look so lonesome up here on this hill all alone . . . all the other flowers grow in clusters in the valley . . . on the other hand, up here you never have to worry about growing in anyone's shadow . . . and you're closer to the sun than they are! But then . . . you have no one to talk to, or to share with . . . I guess that's the price one pays for solitude and independence."[1]

Perhaps because he spent so many hours as a lonely leader of the United Nations, the late Dag Hammarskjold wrote a number of beautiful lines that expressed his feelings.

> What I ask for is absurd: that life shall have a meaning.
> What I strive for is impossible:
>   that my life shall acquire a meaning.
> I dare not believe, I do not see how I shall ever be able
>   to believe: that I am not alone.[2]

One need not be famous, creative, or powerful to be lonely. The condition touches everyone. Yet this fact need not alarm us.

Psychologists speak of "the lonely crowd." Everyone, physically at least, is surrounded or accompanied by people much of the time. At a football game one might be squeezed into a crowd of 10,000 to 70,000 people yet feel no com-

---

1. Reprinted by permission of Universal Press Syndicate.
2. Dag Hammarskjold, *Markings*, trans. Leif Sjoberg and W. H. Auden (New York: Alfred A. Knopf, Inc., 1964)

panionship. He might shout excitedly when there is a great play, but this spirit of oneness is ephemeral. It is a surface spirit. To be lonely in an encompassing crowd is most depressing.

The lonely crowd is found on the New York subway. Going from 116th Street to Times Square, I see the faces of countless other riders. They glance, perhaps, at fellow passengers, but their eyes are uncaring and the glances slip away with no real contact.

Even in your place of business or in your home, you can be all too aware that you really don't know anyone nor does anyone really know you. In my office, I may have appointments, I may be busily searching for photographs, or arranging for illustrations, or participating in meetings and yet receive a sudden jolt when I realize I am truly alone.

The television world seldom portrays this pervasive loneliness. On the screen, men and women vigorously engage in stereotyped symbols of fun, running through fields, strolling on beaches, dancing, singing, riding horses against the setting sun, drinking, lighting cigarettes. Smiling faces with chronically open mouths express gratification with the manifold blessings offered by our culture. Seeing more and more of this, one might observe a bridgeless gap between the fantasies Americans live by and the realities they live in. We know how we are supposed to look when we are happy, what we should do or what we should buy to be happy, to be part of the crowd. But for all this, in our real lives we are lonely.

Children and teen-agers experience periods of feeling alone. "Nobody understands me" is a stock phrase. School psychologists are concerned lest the young person not relate to his peer group. Poetry written by teen-agers deals predominantly with love (or the lack of it), loneliness, and death.

Middle-aged persons find themselves pursuing materialistic goals to a point where they do not notice how lonely they are until their ends are achieved or until failure engulfs them and they have time to look at themselves.

Among the' elderly, loneliness can develop into a real problem, more so than the lack of money, bad as that may be. For example, in a survey taken in Canada recently, 48 percent of the old persons questioned cited loneliness, boredom, and a feeling of being unwanted as their most serious problems.

Consider the Causes

Rejection is one of the major causes of loneliness. Katherine Mansfield's poignant short story of the aging Miss Brill is a classic example of the depression and hurt of being alone that comes from selfish, careless rejection. Miss Brill's one remaining valuable, a fur neckpiece, served as a bulwark against the bleak prospect of growing old with no friends or acquaintances. Her imagination, as she daily stroked and admired the last vestige of better times, finally nerved her to the point where she ventured out into the park to sit on a bench and watch others. She was not the only elderly person so engaged, but somehow she felt she was special because of the fur neckpiece.

As she sat there, she gradually became aware of a young couple at the other end of the bench, obviously annoyed by her presence. They did not care that she could overhear their rude whispers. The girl giggled and ridiculed the neckpiece.

Miss Brill slowly left the park and went back to her lonely room, not even stopping at the baker's to pick up her special Sunday treat of honey buns. She quickly unclasped the fur piece and without looking at it again, put it back into its box. But as she did so, she thought she heard something cry. Imagination could no longer push away loneliness.

Kate and Robert Evans, an outgoing couple in their thirties, moved into a small community, only to learn that small communities can put a damper on the enthusiasm of outsiders. Even in church the barriers were present. When nine-year-old Johnny Evans was to be bused to another school, Kate and Robert did not object, as did their neighbors, who vociferously gathered to stop the procedure. Before long, topics such as civil rights, welfare, and busing tore the community apart. Kate and Robert were left entirely alone. Kate was particularly affected, for her husband commuted to work daily, and she was left to bear the brunt of whispers, stares, and unkind remarks. The community had rejected the Evanses, who learned that standing up for one's principles can cause alienation.

Brad is faced with another kind of loneliness. He and his family firmly believe that people should be free in their life-styles. After a year of college, Brad has dropped out to find himself—who he is, what he believes in, and where he wants to go with his future. Although family and close friends stand by, Brad finds he is suspected of drug abuse and is accused of being a drifter and a confused floater.

The theme of loneliness and rejection is strong in many popular songs. Phonograph records and eight-track tapes have captured the mood, rock ballads tell the story of broken-hearted lovers, adults listen to the blues of the past, and the elderly nostalgically turn memories back to earlier days.

Most of us feel the stir of sympathetic vibrations as we recall the times we loved and found no return of affection, when we volunteered for a responsibility only to be passed by, when we thought we were to be promoted only to see someone else take our place, when we thought an assignment might be coming our way because of our qualifications only to discover someone else getting the nod. To be rejected is painful loneliness.

At least a part of our loneliness can be attributed to the fact that we value our mobility and privacy so much. Paradoxically, the very attainment of this individuality can lead to the feeling that we are indeed facing life alone, dependent only upon ourselves and our own resources.

In earlier generations, husband, wife, and children, together with relatives at times, were closely bound together, often by necessity. The church helped pull family and friends into a unit. House raisings, barn raisings, the harvesting of crops were community affairs. Tools were shared. One knew that if help were necessary, one could count on others. Today we find that many people, in their desire for privacy or because of geographical distance from families, are alone.

Unavoidable family circumstances lead to loneliness. Husbands or wives die, children grow up and marry or move away, families are transferred to distant places because of employment. Even short-term separations because of illness or travel contribute to the feeling that one is by oneself, with little to look forward to but long evenings before the television set or radio, and the silence when the programs end.

Self-Defeating Solutions

How can we face being alone? The following suggestions tend to lead to more isolation in the end, even though they temporarily fill the time. Unfortunately, these solutions are frequently resorted to.

1. Lose yourself in work. You will be busy. Haul more work home at night from the classroom or office.
2. Participate frantically in more leisure activites. Play more golf or tennis. Jog every morning and evening, not so much for your health as to escape loneliness. Go on camping vacations and cruises. Purchase a second home.

3. Perhaps a drink *or several* will help. But usually, as time goes by, more and more drinks are needed.
4. See an analyst. He may discover some quirk in your background that has created loneliness. There may be something or someone else to blame.
5. Read books on how to be more positive in your thinking. If you believe loneliness is not there, perhaps it will disappear. Count your blessings and rationalize the loneliness.
6. Succumb to self-pity. Attempt to get others to pity you by pouring•out those lonely feelings. Or tell yourself, "It's no use," and give up.

Positive Ways to Handle Loneliness

Paradoxically, the first suggestion is to be alone. While we may fear loneliness, we can relieve it by facing ourselves for a while—away from the crowd, the co-workers, the family. Loneliness is a matter of attitude. We must look ourselves in the eye and see our lives in the proper perspective. Physical aloneness is a necessity at times. The late Episcopal Bishop James Pike once said, "We are meant to have some life with ourselves, and there is a kind of loneliness that besieges us if we are denied it."

In taking a good look at ourselves and attempting a bit of self-analysis, we will no doubt find a great deal of self-pity. In congregations, I have noted that about 90 percent of those who complain of being left alone are the self-pitiers. They shut themselves in and their friends out, all the while complaining that they are lonely. Eventually, people begin to avoid such individuals, and the world passes them by. Like the caterpillars, they spin cocoons around themselves—but make no attempt to break out as butterflies.

Excessive self-sufficiency is another ingredient for loneliness. A prominent church member in a congregation I served once told me it took a serious illness followed by surgery to open his eyes to the fact that he really needed others. Illness, war, death—all have a way of forcing us to appreciate so many things we have taken for granted. Sometimes our self-pride prevents our realizing how much we actually depend on others; we feel we must not ask for their help, nor should we accept it if it is offered. It may be more blessed to give than to receive, but there are times when it is important to know how to receive willingly and graciously.

We may combat our own loneliness by drawing closer to others who are lonely. Individuals who have gone through an experience are the very ones to understand and help others in the same situation, thus making a wider circle full of fresh interests for all concerned.

Involving oneself in genuinely seeking the betterment of others draws one away from self-pity and broadens one's horizons. A friend of mine was grief-stricken when she received a telegram from the Pentagon informing her that one of her two sons was lost on a mission training flight near the Philippines. His plane had presumably crashed into the sea, but was never found. She and her husband unashamedly wept. As if this were not enough, her husband died shortly thereafter of a heart attack. Two deaths in the immediate family within a short time could have driven my friend into her own cocoon of loneliness.

However, in a world of desperate need, she did not shrink from others. Rather she became active in raising funds for black colleges. New challenges opened up to her. She became involved in still other philanthropic programs. Over a period of time, she learned to know herself better. She asked, "What have I to give to others?" Her acceptance of life shows that with all its richness and variety, its terror and its zaniness, life goes on and we are a part of it.

LONELINESS

Prayer is a means of overcoming loneliness. Such a statement may sound naïve. We cannot offer prayer as a panacea for all of the world's ills and let it go at that. But prayer can be a way through which help can come if we keep in mind that prayer is God affirming life. Through true prayer, one cannot be lonely because his life is bound up with the lives of countless others everywhere. Intercessory prayer, prayer for others, has been called the most ancient friendship of all believers. For those who have known loneliness, prayer is the way by which a person can be brought back to life.

In the church I now attend, we have a prayer tree. Every Sunday after the service, those who wish can write a prayer and hang it on one of the branches. These prayers are then picked by the ministers and become a part of the prayer at the next Sunday service. The fellowship of prayer binds us into one, and we recognize in the prayers of others the needs of our own hearts.

Even Christ experienced loneliness. William Stringfellow, lawyer, author, and theologian, has pointed out that few greeted, few honored, few understood, few loved him; few celebrated his vocation. People shouted for his death. Yet his words rang out, "You shall all flee and leave me alone, and yet I am not alone, for my father is with me."

Much of our loneliness is a spiritual vacuum, which we try to fill with work, leisure activities, drink, drugs, sex, medicine, a shallow form of positive thinking, or self-pity. We may search for crowds only to find we are still lonely.

Our need is to turn to that companion who never quite leaves us alone and friendless. God is close by. When we come to this reality, our lives will change, and we will find that living, no matter where, is filled with wonder and goodness. We still may find ourselves trapped in places we find unpleasant, and life may seem without joy, but the stars do shine. We are created as delicate instruments of a God who loves us.

Healing Helps

1. Go where the action is, or bring it where you are. People are not going to spend time looking you up. Put on the teakettle, knock on doors, and invite people to your house.
2. Talk to your friend, minister, or counselor about your loneliness, but be willing to listen to him as well. Don't continue to feel sorry for yourself.
3. Set aside some time for your own self. Solitude can be helpful in giving you a new perspective.
4. Cultivate your best resources. You will find that you are welcome among others when they learn what talents, personality, and gifts you possess. (And we all possess them in some degree!)
5. Be cheerful, for people tend to be as cheerful as those around them. A long face or self-pitying tone only serves to drive others away.
6. Remember that God is always with you; he is your friend, so you are never truly alone.

UNHAPPINESS

Brighten Your Outlook

Unhappiness is a rather vague term, yet it encompasses so many little indefinite sore spots that the person who achieves true happiness is in an enviable position. Happiness, then, becomes an important part of the healing process.

When asked to write down what they considered happiness to be, a small group with whom I meet came up with a variety of definitions. A few of them are:

> Happiness is a cool drink of water on a hot summer day.
>
> Happiness is greeting your family after a long absence.
>
> Happiness is bringing a recovered patient home from the hospital.
>
> Happiness is love.
>
> Happiness is a telephone call from someone you love.
>
> Happiness is knowing God is not far away.

Everyone can add definitions of his own, for happiness has many connotations. It is a state of well-being, comfort, delight, satisfaction, bliss, enjoyment, pleasure, success. On a bumper sticker I read that Happiness is skiing. I was pleased to observe, in a major magazine, that Happiness is being bald.

It would appear that happiness is on tap for us to reach for and own. Actually, however, the keys to happiness must be earned. To enjoy the happiness we seek, we must understand these keys, use them, then pass the knowledge on to others.

In a "Peanuts" cartoon drawn by Charles M. Schulz, we see Linus with his ever-present security blanket and Charlie Brown sitting on the curb. Charlie asks, "What's that dotted line on the blanket for, Linus?" Linus proceeds to tear the blanket in half; then he offers one part to Charlie. He says, "Happiness should be shared!"[1]

Cultivate key attitudes that enable you to recognize the best in life, then share them with others.

Trust Yourself and Others

One of my favorite singers is Terry Jacks, and I especially enjoy hearing his album *Seasons in the Sun*. One evening, I decided to replay "Sail Away," but I inadvertently pushed the playing arm and scratched the record. The beautiful music is still on the record, but so is the flaw.

Resentment is like the flaw; so is suspicion. These unpleasant emotions cut across the beauty of relationships. As with the music, the relationships are still there, but they are marred. We don't intend to deface the love and friendship we value but somehow we do.

How do we go about finding help in coping with our resentment and suspicion? Assistance may be right at our fingertips, but we fail to recognize it. Carl Sandburg, in

1. Text from *Peanuts* by Charles M. Schulz; © 1956, 1963 United Feature Syndicate, Inc.

UNHAPPINESS

Always the Young Strangers, writes of John Standish, former president of Lombard College, who harbored extreme resentment against the school. "He may have been wronged by Lombard," records Sandburg. "Somehow I never found the time to really look into what happened. I merely knew that he read a thousand important books in several different languages, that he lectured to hundreds of teachers' institutes on how to educate the young, that he traveled three times around the planet Earth, that he loved trees and did a work with trees, for which I am infinitely grateful, that somehow all his travels and reading and love of trees couldn't help him when his heart nursed a hate."

Harboring resentment and not giving others the benefit of the doubt when there have been unpleasant situations can only result in unhappiness—for the one doing the resenting. Such resentment may be with us from the time we arise in the morning until we go to bed at night; sometimes it is with us in our dreams.

One of my minister friends admitted he resented going to church council meetings, for whenever he went, one particular member always wanted to know exactly how many calls he had made on prospective members during the past month. "And when I don't come through with a good-sized group of new members, John reminds me that Arvin, pastor of the church a few blocks away, is packing them in." It reached the point where my friend could barely get himself to make any calls at all and always appeared late at the council meetings, thus compounding his woes.

If we think our supervisor at work shows favoritism to one particular member of the staff, we harbor resentment, and our bitterness makes us unhappy. We may mentally create great put-down scenes or write imaginary letters, but our emotional upset is not relieved. An employee may learn that a colleague is receiving a higher salary than he is for no greater amount of work and sizzle inwardly. He may slack off in his work, but he still is not happy.

Resentment rears its ugly head when we feel left out of social groups, decision-making meetings, status-symbol parties or dinners. Women may resent having to stay home with the children; men may resent having no time to themselves on weekends. Commuters seethe when the train is not on time or the bus runs into an unusual amount of traffic. There seems to be no end to individual causes for resentment.

Mass resentment may manifest itself. When Dan Devine, former coach of the Green Bay Packers, did not produce a championship team as Vince Lombardi used to do, he and his family were subjected to harassment. Whole neighborhoods may resent certain families moving into what they consider "their" area.

Listening to both sides of the situation and honestly trying to give the other party the benefit of the doubt can go a long way toward alleviating the problem. A friend of mine told me how she resented the way a teacher in the local school was treating her son. It had reached the point where the boy was miserable both at home and at school. His parents were also upset. I suggested that she try to resolve the situation by trusting the teacher and, in this case, give her the benefit of the doubt by going to speak with her. The feelings now being expressed were helping no one, least of all the boy. As it turned out, the boy needed to be challenged in the quality of his work; he was simply bored in class and showed it. The teacher had misunderstood the reason for his attitude and resented it. After a month had passed, I saw the mother again. Her attitude was one of delight. Her son had won an award for an extra project. The festering problem had cleared up and a new rapport prevailed between the boy, together with his family, and the teacher.

If we work from the premise that the other person is

basically good and trustworthy, we will find things to bear out that premise. This is not a matter of blind trust or foolish confidence. A Pollyannaish attitude is not the answer. We must use good judgment, to be sure, but that judgment must be tempered with trust rather than with resentment and suspicion.

Live in the Now

Lamenting decisions of the past brings unhappiness. I am sure I could make myself miserable in this way. Two of the responsibilities that I enjoy are photography and writing. But many years were spent in the parish ministry, during which I did not pursue these activities except as hobbies. Perhaps if I had studied only photography or journalism I might today have a more prestigious job in either of these fields. Presidential photographers have exciting lives. Or how about the photojournalists for various well-known magazines? Surely they are living life to the fullest. No commuting for them.

But I have come to realize that the past is merely a passport to the present and the future. In my association with the people in my parishes and with the church as a whole, I learned a great deal that is of value to me today. I cannot change the past but I can build on it.

A prosperous engineer asked, "Where am I?" He wasn't concerned with his geographical position. Rather, after fifty-five years of living, he was concerned with what he was now doing with his life. He had reached a point where he felt that apparent success was not enough. What contribution was he making to life now?

The present is what we are living in, not the past. As Mrs. Lyndon B. Johnson said when questioned about her feelings on the subject, "It's [the past] there to savor, to bring out around a fire with a few old friends. But it can't be the meat of daily living. You can't feed on it."

The Bible instructs us to live for the present and anchor our future in it. Christ said, "Therefore do not be anxious about tomorrow, for tomorrow will be anxious for itself. Let the day's own trouble be sufficient for the day." (Matt. 6:34) Our major efforts should be devoted to getting the most from our present twenty-four hours.

Roll with the Punches

A young friend stopped by one day as I was working on the lawn. I needed the break, so we sat down together on the steps to talk. Eventually, we finished the conversation about the weather and politics and got around to talking about his home, his responsibilities. "You know," he said earnestly, "I would be a lot happier if I just had more money. If I could double my income, I'd be walking on air!"

I asked him what made him think more money was the answer.

"Oh," he replied, "I'd like to give Nancy the comforts she wants. I could have all the stereo equipment I'd like. And we could travel, go to Broadway plays, eat out more often, take the kids places. Man! That's what I want!"

We think if we only had more money we would automatically be happy. But one has only to read the papers, listen to the radio, or turn on TV to see the error of such reasoning. Contentment does not increase proportionately with possessions. Actually, the amount of money one has is not the deciding factor. Low-income people can be very happy, and persons with all sorts of material wealth most unhappy. The opposite can also be true. Many poor people are not content while some wealthy ones are. No, money is not a panacea.

UNHAPPINESS

In times of recession, to be out of a job and unable to meet payments on the house or provide adequate food for the family can truly take on the aspects of tragedy. But circumstances need not destroy us. We can roll with the punches. The opponent levels what could be a lethal punch, but we can roll away from it and, while it may land, it does not do irrevocable damage.

When I was a boy during the depression of the thirties, my father was out of work for two entire years. He could not make payments on his loans. We lost all our property except the home we lived in and there was a constant threat of foreclosure on that. We hauled logs from the woods nearby to burn in the furnace. A nickel's worth of soup bones were boiled to make our main course. Occasionally we had potatoes seasoned with paprika. An orange was a gift at Christmas. Despite all this, unpleasant as it was, I would say we were a happy family.

The happy person has learned to live and accept what comes, building on that instead of bemoaning his fate. He has found the golden mean between competition and cooperation. He does not run away but stands and fights. But the fight is constructive, not destructive. It leads to further growth and development.

A Hollywood celebrity recalled her life of emotional defeats, unhappy romances, twice-broken marriages. She went through a period of mental depression. At last one day she said to her doctor, "I have to get well because sometime I must win. I just can't lose forever." The statement proved to be the turning point of her life. She began to climb out of her deep depression, saying to herself, "I know I will get over this." Facing the facts led to a new confidence. She later explained her new-found happiness and peace of mind. "I had to turn my mind around, see myself as I was, to respond to whatever element in my life that promised happiness for that particular day."

Strength comes when we strive to overcome obstacles and win the fight. The important thing to remember is that we need not go the route alone. Why should we live in our inadequate strength when we have God's power at hand? All we need do is ask for that help; he will give it.

Crawl Out of Your Shell

Seeing me outside with my camera, my neighbor brought over a turtle which his son kept as a pet. "Look at the markings," he said. "He'd make a good subject for a picture."

We set the old warrior down in the grass, but he merely pulled in his head and legs and that was it. We waited patiently. Finally when the turtle judged the danger to be past, he cautiously stuck out first his head and then his legs. As I tried to focus my micro-lens on his head, he lurched away, bent on escape.

When we are under emotional stress, when we are sad, when we are lonely, when we are alarmed, we tend to act like that turtle. We retreat into our shells, closing out everything and everybody. If such retreat would improve our spirits and make us happy, that would be one thing. But such is not the case. Retreating within ourselves only brings more unhappiness.

One way to come out of our self-imposed shells is to do some sort of service for the good of others, not just once, but frequently.

Every tenth year, a great New York surgeon makes it a practice to go overseas to some area of the world where doctors are needed and spends one year in service to others. A dentist friend of mine spends a month, his vacation time, every five or six years offering his time and services to South American people who are too poor to have their teeth taken care of otherwise. Various persons in the arts devote hours to bringing a new outlook to the disadvantaged. The persons who have been involved in this giving of time and talent have broadened their horizons and expressed an increased zest for living.

Not everyone can be a great surgeon, a practicing dentist, or talented in the arts. But we all have something we can use to enhance the lives of others, to bring courage, hope, and happiness to family, friends, neighbors, and even people we do not know.

Set Realistic Goals

Realistic goals are neither low nor easy goals. Being realistic does not rob them of their challenge, their ability to spur us on. But they are not impossible. They are worthy goals which lead to better things, not antagonism and frustration and bitterness. If you constantly are aware of a great gap between anticipated and actual achievement, you can narrow that gap by assessing your capabilities realistically and adjusting the demands you make on yourself.

Let us consider goals we set in our day-to-day living. I have often found unhappiness in planning to accomplish more in a given time than is physically possible. There are so many things I want to do, so many things that need to be done. I found myself listing all these projected activities, especially those to be done over a weekend—photographing some leaves I've been keeping in the refrigerator, repairing several loose rungs on some antique chairs, hanging the pictures, working on an article, and the like. The standard joke at our house has been that a job I proclaim will take "only an hour" takes most of the day, and "only a few minutes" duty consumes several hours. I decided my goals had been unrealistic.

To correct the problem, I have tried the "job jar" approach, à la Dagwood Bumstead. All the little things that need to be done are listed on pieces of paper, which are folded and placed in an old goldfish bowl to be drawn out at random. I may not get everything done, but at least I have not made so many demands on myself.

Priority as well as time enters the picture. Are there certain aims which are more important to us than others? Sometimes a goal must be altered or even abandoned in favor of a still better one. Psychiatrists have told us there is no top or bottom to life. There is that in-between where we must find a place where our capabilities fit. This applies to the goals we set for ourselves.

John D. Rockefeller III has correctly said that the road to happiness lies in two simple principles. The first is to find what it is that interests you that you can do well. When you find it, put your whole soul into it—every bit of energy and ambition and natural ability you have.

Learn to Believe

In a sermon at one of his revivals, Billy Graham told his listeners of his search for contented and happy men in his world travels. He said, "I have found such persons where Christ has been personally and decisively received. There is only one permanent way to have peace of soul that wells up in joy, contentment, and happiness and that is to believe in Christ."

To believe in someone bigger than yourself is another secret of happiness. Terry Bradshaw, quarterback of the world football champions, the Pittsburgh Steelers, had drifted away from Christ. In the spring of 1974 he was divorced by his wife, and in training camp he lost his starting position. Everything seemed to be going wrong for him.

UNHAPPINESS

"One day I was sitting in my apartment, and I got kind of choked up," Bradshaw told the press. "I could not take it any more. I decided to get back to it . . . go back to reading the Bible. Everybody needs to believe in something. Things go bad, you go someplace, to somebody." Bradshaw said the problems of his divorce and his performance on the field were compounded by his inability to tap the faith he had leaned on since his youth. "I'd gotten away from it, and that bothered me. I said to myself, 'Shoot! I can't handle this alone!'"

Following such a facing-up to himself, he found his personality and play on the field improved. His coach called his performance against the Buffalo Bills in a playoff game Bradshaw's finest. "I'm not saying that I'm playing better because of my getting back to my faith," said Bradshaw. "It's just something I believe in.".

We all believe in something, whether it be power, money, prestige, or personal growth. We are usually willing to work for these things. But there is a difference in the way unhappy and happy persons approach their beliefs. The unhappy person thinks only of himself. Too much of the world is on the wrong scent in the pursuit of happiness, as Henry Drummond aptly put it. They think happiness is in having and getting and being served by others.

The happy person has outstripped his foundering friends by finding happiness in giving and serving others. As a matter of fact, the happy person dedicates himself to those things that are bigger than he is. He finds in happiness more than the joy of eating and drinking. His happiness comes from obligations that are fulfilled, duty which has been discharged, acts of generosity done secretly, and appreciation of the beautiful in nature, art, and conduct. The happy person is one who believes that life is good despite setbacks and frustrations and then works to make his belief a reality.

Healing Helps

If faithfully followed, these seven helps should go a long way toward cultivating and maintaining happiness.

1. Appreciate blessings and forget about those things you do not have and cannot acquire.
2. Understand the importance of things more valuable than money.
3. Live and enjoy the present.
4. Accept what cannot be changed.
5. Work toward a realistic but challenging goal.
6. Consider others; help them when they need it.
7. Think optimistically.

During the next week, keep a written record of examples of the ways you have fulfilled these suggestions.

ANGER

 ## *So You've Blown Your Top!*

The violent argument, punctuated by the loud slamming of doors, could be heard throughout the normally quiet suburban neighborhood in the early summer evening. It wasn't long before an upstairs window opened, and many articles of apparel were hurled out, followed by an empty suitcase. Children could be heard crying inside the house. In a short time, the door of a car slammed and, leaving his belongings strewn over the lawn, the husband backed violently out of the driveway. He never saw the car that hit him broadside. He wasn't killed, but he will always be paralyzed from the waist down as a result of the accident. He and his wife live with the knowledge that their display of anger which left such lasting consequences was over a relatively simple incident.

As we have seen, the simple process of losing one's temper can lead to far-reaching consequences. In a less dramatic but nonetheless tragic case, a husband's wife left him. Later he admitted sadly, "It's mainly my fault. I have a bad temper. I love her dearly, but as I look back now I can understand why she didn't realize it."

The hostile drive of anger finds expression in many ways, and all too often it leads to injury, divorce or separation, crime, and delinquency. And this same hostile drive seems to be on the upsurge with the constant rise of the number of violent crimes in all segments of society. Even a person who claims he has never lost his temper can suffer as a result of anger kept too tightly under control, seething beneath the surface like a festering boil. Anger has a bearing on personalities and interrelationships, adjustments to daily situations, and getting what we want from life. We all have our moments of anger, whether expressed or not, obvious or hidden. Anger is a most human emotion.

In this chapter on the sore spot of anger, we will think about the dangers of anger and yet realize that there are times when anger actually can be good for us. Constructive ways of dealing with anger help in the healing process.

Dangers in Anger

When we become angry and lose our tempers, we may not realize the damage we are doing to ourselves. A mental chemist could tell us how our mental state affects our physical being. Discord in the mind produces discord in the body and emotions such as anger can easily get out of hand and poison our bodies.

An expert in psychosomatic medicine at Harvard University tells what happens in our bodies when we blow our top. Respiration deepens; the heart beats more rapidly; the arterial pressure rises; the blood shifts from the stomach and intestines to the heart, the central nervous system, and the muscles; the processes of the alimentary canal cease; sugar is freed from reserves in the liver; the spleen contracts and discharges its contents of concentrated corpuscles; and adrenalin is secreted from the adrenal medulla.

Just imagine all those things happening just because one is angry! More obvious signs of which we are aware are a flushed face, swollen neck veins, clenched fists, and sometimes temporary loss of speech. In some cases, vision becomes blurred because anger has blocked off the visual centers of the brain. Such physical responses could easily be the cause of industrial, automobile, and home accidents.

Investigators have linked rage to a wide range of physical ailments. My doctor verified what we all suspect. While a person may not show any of the aforementioned outward physical signs of anger, suppressed rage can be even more damaging in the long run. It has been linked to hypertension, asthma, migraine and other headaches, colitis, some thyroid disorders, and certain types of arthritis. Frequently, it has been known to bring on attacks of angina pectoris.

A ten-year study by doctors at Cornell University shows that many causes of nose ailments—other than getting punched by someone during a fit of anger—such as sinusitis and colds have coincided with intense emotional upheavals. In some persons, anger results in a sharp pain in the back; in others, a splitting headache, indigestion, loss of appetite, and various nervous ailments.

The interesting aspect about these studies is that so many people still refuse to connect emotions with physical condition, though certainly many articles and books have pointed it out frequently. In some cases, the Cornell researchers found they could turn symptoms of patients on and off merely by referring to the object of their anger. One man suffered an asthmatic attack at the mere mention of his wife.

Many of us carry deeply hidden rage from infancy and childhood. As babies we had hunger and needs which on occasion could not or should not have been satisfied by our mothers. Even an infant can be observed crying and turning red from frustration. Small children may vent their rage in temper tantrums, only to be punished by the adult world, with resulting fear.

The process has become frustration, anger, punishment, fear. Gradually we are conditioned to connect anger and fear as stimulus and effect. Later in life, when a situation realistically demands firmness or aggressiveness on our part, we may tend to suppress our anger because we are afraid to vent it. We must now learn that no one will punish us for the legitimate expression of self-assertiveness, as our parents once punished us for undisciplined temper tantrums.

Another primary source of anger is a feeling of inferiority or inadequacy. Some psychiatrists believe a feeling of infantile dependence is difficult to outgrow. In our adult lives, few of us can get from husband, wife, co-workers, or friends the treatment we had or wanted from our parents. If, in addition, we have been overprotected or forced too soon on our own, we may recoil from independence. Such faulty conditioning may make us into adults who, regardless of physical size or intellectual capacity, still crave the support which cannot be gratified in adult life. The result is anger.

There is an illustration demonstrating this cycle. A young man was sent to college. While there, he was angry with everyone—his professors, his classmates, and even his girl friend. He left school and went to work to "find himself." But he fared no better on the job. He quit several, never satisfied. Finally, an employer took a personal interest in him. He liked the young man despite his attitude and at last persuaded him to go to the company psychiatrist for an interview. The visit disclosed that the young man's parents had been divorced when he was very young and he had been reared by his mother and older sister, who pampered him, praised him, and acted as buffers for all the blows from the outside world. Away from this protective environment, he could not cope. He resented the fact that his mother and sister now insisted he try to wrestle with his own problems, but at the same time he felt inferior to his more capable friends. The damage to his already delicate self-esteem enraged him. He projected his anger onto others, claiming they were hostile and persecutory toward him. Without treatment, these dynamics might have eventually pushed him into severe paranoia or criminal acts.

Anger runs the gamut from maladjustment to everyday life to emotion symptomatic of severe mental illness. Many of us have unconscious anger within us. Some people are chronically angry, constantly have a chip on their shoulder. Such conditions could be brought on by physiological problems. We all know that if we are hungry, we tend to be irritable. How often have we felt the flush of anger while sitting in a restaurant where the service has been poor or unusually slow? How much more intense is our feeling when poor service is combined with a deadline to make an appointment or to get back to work. Annoyance with the delay is coupled with a sense of fear regarding the results of that delay.

When we suffer from a headache, an upset stomach, a bad cold, sunburn, poison ivy, or any such physical disorder, we tend to be on edge, mean, intolerant, snappish, or less gracious than usual. When anger is continuous, it might be well for us to seek the cause very seriously. Perhaps we are not in the best of physical condition and a medical examination is in order.

Psychological factors may also lead to our frequently blowing our top. We may have such a low opinion of ourselves that we are uncomfortable around others, as if the proximity to them would take something away from our already negligible ego. We may feel abused and used by others, denied life. In such a frame of mind, we would have a tendency to express our desire for emotional distance through anger.

The environment in which a person has lived affects his response to others. In some cases, conflict has been the only means of communication. Arguments at school, work, play, or in the home are the only means of expression and emotional stimulation. Even affection is brought out through what might seem like anger to persons accustomed to a quieter, more orderly life.

We once lived next door to a couple who had both come from "violent" backgrounds, as described in the preceding paragraph. It was a conflict marriage. For some time we were concerned over their violent, loud arguments. Once we were even startled to hear shattering glass and see a pan coming through the kitchen window. Strange as it seemed to us, this couple was happy, or at least they said they were. Unfortunately, such violence of emotions can be disastrous where children are concerned or if firearms are handy. How often do we read about tragedies where a man or woman has killed the one he claimed to love because his anger finally went too far.

There is also an anger labeled "sadness anger." We all know what it is to be sad. The loss of a loved one, a friend, or a pet can bring on the painful emotion. In such times, anger is easier for us to vent. So we express our anger at the time of sadness toward the hospital, nurses, fate, circumstances, doctors, even God. Sadness is an inner emotion so we sublimate it into an outer emotion such as anger. This sadness anger is a persistent problem facing marriage counselors. After the initial phase of the honeymoon, a wife may confess, "John has such an uncontrollable temper. He never displayed it before we were married, but petty things upset him. He doesn't think our sex life is fulfilling." Later we hear, "He spanks the children needlessly. Insignificant things lead him to shout and rave. I just can't stand it any more!"

The fantasies of married life vanish like bursting bubbles, little by little. The ideal of the perfect spouse, the constant good times, the perfect companionship—all seem gone.

Sadness at losing or giving up these dreams or ideals is painful. Such crises may arise numerous times during a marriage.

The causes of anger are manifold, and the results of anger can be unpleasant, damaging, disastrous. Anger is explosive and can set off numerous chain reactions.

Helpful Anger

Yet anger can have its positive side as well. Before condemning entirely this volatile emotion, let us consider times when anger can be a good thing.

Carl Sandburg, one of the biographers of Abraham Lincoln, writes that when he was a young man the future president made a trip down the Mississippi to New Orleans with a cargo of produce. After disposing of the cargo, Lincoln and a fellow boatman wandered about the city. They came upon a slave market, the first Lincoln had ever seen. There he observed people being sold to the highest bidder, families broken apart, human beings regarded as animals. Lincoln, it is reported, witnessed the event with horror, which changed to anger. He said to his companion, "If I ever get the chance to hit that thing, I'll hit it hard!"

I confess I was not paying too much attention at an unusually boring church meeting. Droning discussions on salaries, the fuel bill, and the hiring of a new custodian failed to enliven me. Occasionally, when someone suggested a new program or action, I did enter into the discussion but, unfortunately, such suggestions led to nothing being decided and they were tabled for future consideration. Glancing at my watch, I was glad to note that the meeting surely must end soon.

For a few moments, my imagination went on a journey of its own. I seemed to see a man who stepped forward, dressed neatly and cleanly enough, but obviously upset. He strode forward, his face flushed. He turned and faced the assembled church men and women. "I'm sick and tired of you people! You are hyprocrites! You talk as if you love each other here, but I've heard you cut each other to pieces behind a guise of friendship. You're afraid to take any kind of action that would amount to anything worthwhile. You condemn those who are not as you are. You look alive, but you're dead inside; your church is dead. You are like the scribes and Pharisees!"

Abruptly I came out of my reverie. The meeting was over. A few people glanced at me curiously as I sat there. I could not help thinking how Christ had become angry with the events and actions of the church of his day. His anger came through in phrases such as "you blind guides . . . you blind men . . . you are like whitewashed tombs which appear beautiful, but within they are full of dead men's bones and all uncleanness . . . you serpents, you brood of vipers!" (Matt. 23:16, 27, 29)

What do we do with the angry Jesus? Was he showing righteous indignation? Or can we say that anger is a legitimate part of man's personality and can have a creative and cleansing use?

Because a person rarely demonstrates his anger outwardly does not necessarily mean he is a well-balanced personality; he may merely be inhibited. He may be afraid to show his anger. He may not even have any strong feeling about worthwhile things. As Lincoln and Christ illustrate, there are times when anger is creative and helpful.

We might wish for more anger in the right places. Few things are more satisfying than an angry taxpayer registering his disgust at the polls because of the way his money is wasted by municipal, state, or national governments.

Some of our greatest men have been angry men. The Boston Tea Party was planned and executed by angry men protesting what they strongly felt to be an injustice. Laws have been changed because enough people became angry with inequities under the old ones.

While some may become incoherent in the heat of anger, others have found in the emotion a power to transmit their ideas with unusual forcefulness and clarity. Such was the case, it is said by close associates, of Dwight D. Eisenhower. When aroused, he spoke in prose flowing with a smooth beauty and grammatical precision entirely lacking in his more relaxed moments. While Harry Truman was one of our more talkative presidents, his remarks made in anger are the ones which have become classics. A well-known newspaper editor was normally a conversational bore, but when one of his correspondents made a stupid mistake or the wire services were late in delivering an important story, the man would hold his audience, whoever happened to be at hand, spellbound with invective, whether directed at a vice-president whose company had sent him a garbled message or a mere stringer who had misspelled a name. Anger was his high octane fuel for getting material correct.

Times for righteous indignation abound. There is so much in the world about which we should become aroused, and we can make a point and win a decision through the constructive use of anger.

We can express frustration in a cleansing moment of anger. In a sermon, the Reverend James Gilliom told about a church member hurrying to catch a bus at New York's Port Authority Terminal during rush hour. When the walk light turned green, the church member and the crowd of people behind him were about to step into the street when yet another car moved around the corner, blocking everyone's path. The church member happened to be carrying a furled umbrella. Before he realized it, he had hit the car a good whack across its hood. He looked with astonishment at the man in the car, and after a moment they both grinned.

A certain amount of aggressive energy is normal and manageable in adulthood and we should not repress it. We have need to let off steam and "whack the car across the hood" when we feel we have a right to do so. Bottled-up rage can take both physical and mental toll on us. Naturally, this is no excuse to be constantly lashing out at friends, family, or employer in order to prevent getting high blood pressure. What it does mean is use anger rather than let it use you.

Tempers are like runaway horses; they can take you where you do not want to go unless they are controlled. Consider the story of the hot-tempered Irishman so given to anger and profanity that the foreman on his construction crew warned him the next time he had an outburst of such a nature, he would be fired on the spot. Things went fine most of the morning until a clumsy iron worker overhead dropped a hot rivet on the back of the Irishman's neck. Howling in pain and anger, he looked up and was about to address a few well-chosen remarks to the riveter when he saw the foreman approaching. Hastily editing his eloquence, he glared up at the culprit and said, "Charles, *do* be more careful!"

Dorothea Dix, angered by inhumanity in mental hospitals, brought about a change. An angry Billy Mitchell crusaded for an air force. An aroused citizenry struggled together for the end of the Vietnam war. A few individuals, realizing that pollution can destroy all of us, work to clean up the atmosphere and waterways.

From our anger, creative thoughts and drive can result. We do much shadowboxing in our relationships. We hide our feelings and others hide theirs from us. Through honest expression we can clear the way for a new relationship.

Some things we must be angry about so that the spirit of life will have a chance to grow in us and in the world. There are times, however, when we need help in channeling our own anger and in dealing with anger in others so that there may be constructive rather than destructive results.

How to Handle Anger in Others

When we meet anger in others, it is necessary for us to take certain steps. By following some practical suggestions, we help turn this strong emotion into a beneficial tool. Consider these ideas.

1. *Maintain your own calm.* A measure of self-control will prevent the disastrous action of meeting anger with anger. In asking "What can I do about this situation?" we are on the way to self-control. The brain rather than the emotions is needed here.
2. *Use humor.* This does *not* mean laughing at the person or group being confronted. Such action would only serve to make matters worse. Rather, try to find, if possible, something humorous in the situation, or even in yourself, thus deflecting the anger.
3. *Don't force your opponent out on a limb.* The first impulse in an argument is to try to win it. Strike mediator Theodore Kheel, however, has said that one of his main tasks in bringing parties together is to keep one from backing the other into a corner. "One of the ways I do this," he says, "is to bring both parties in a dispute gradually up to a point where I suggest a solution. As soon as I tell them this, I change the subject. I may talk about anything I can think of so as to give them time to think about the solution. Then I

draw out their reactions to my solution." In this way, face-losing reactions are avoided.

4. *Respect the other person's integrity.* People have a tendency to ridicule the anger of others as one means of fighting them. Such goading only brings about further extremes of action.

5. *Seek help.* When confronted by a person who has a tendency to be chronically angry, realize that he may need medical or even legal advice. In the case of threatened violence, it may be necessary to call the police to protect all parties concerned. The peacekeeping authorities may prove to be a better deterent than well-meaning friends or relatives.

How to Handle Anger in Yourself

Most of us are aware of the rising feeling of anger. When we are conscious of such emotion, we would be wise to avoid throwing our mouths into gear before our brains are engaged. Here are some suggestions to think about:

1. *Allow for a cooling-off period.* The cliché "count to ten" has practical value. In ice hockey when a player is penalized, he is sent to the penalty box to cool off. His teammates must then play without him. This cooling off may take on several different forms for those of us not involved in playing hockey. We may suggest a coffee break before continuing the argument, agreeing not to talk about the subject under discussion for that period of time. We may try to set some ground rules or basic ideas in which we are in agreement. If we are alone, we may consciously try to think about something else for a brief period of time.

2. *Let off steam in some form of physical activity.* One good way is through vigorous physical sports and exercise such as tennis, handball, basketball, jogging, or even rope-jumping. My son Joel, upon finding he had carelessly ruined several expensive pieces of wood while putting together a grandfather clock, necessitating the purchase of more such pieces, took his anger with himself out by pounding nails into a 2x4 piece of wood. One homemaker I know takes out her anger with herself or others by plunging vigorously into a window- and floor-cleaning spree.

3. *Try writing letters expressing your anger.* The writer, Max Beerbohm, made a habit of dreaming up and writing letters as his outlet for anger. He never sent those letters, but in the process of writing them he would come to see how silly and foolish his reasons were, and his anger evaporated.

4. *Attempt to pinpoint the cause of your anger.* The most obvious cause is not necessarily the real cause for upset feelings. There is a tendency to transfer hostilities from one area to another, only serving to spread the anger and certainly not getting to the root of it. What is the *real* reason for your anger?

5. *Don't be ashamed to share the fact that you become angry* with a qualified neutral observer such as a counselor or minister. Frequently, just talking about the anger will help dissipate it or at least lead to a solution or different per-spective. A physical checkup by the family physician would not be a bad suggestion.

6. *Realize that anger is not unusual.* But to be angry with the right person, to the right degree, at the right time, for the right purpose, and in the right way is the difficulty which must be dealt with. The ability to keep cool in a crisis is not an inherent one, but through patience it can be acquired.

Healing Helps

1. Keep an "anger diary" for a week. Write down:
   a. What prompted your anger?
   b. How long did your anger last?
   c. How did you resolve your cause for anger?
   d. Did your anger do any good—for anyone?
2. Did you find that:
   a. Most of your causes for anger were petty and meaningless?
   b. No one benefited by your anger, not even you?
   c. Afterward you were sorry your emotional outburst took place?
3. Consider the meaning of these statements:
   a. Never forget what a man says to you when he is angry.
   b. A little pot boils easily.
   c. Anger is a stone thrown at a wasps' nest.

INDECISION

4

Right Now Is a Good Time

Decisions—decisions—decisions. Trivial, irrevocable, unimportant, tentative, vital, joyous, forceful, dreaded, compelling, casual—all kinds of decisions face us in our lifetimes, in our daily living. Some decisions we can delay, but others defy procrastination. How can we be guided so that we do not make too many wrong choices? What attitude is necessary in facing the inevitability of all those selections confronting us?

Some people appear decisive by nature. They have no apparent difficulty in determining at once the way they should go, the choices they should make. Even occasional errors in judgment do not deter them. On the other hand, some poor souls cringe from the very idea of making a choice and encourage others to control their lives by their very indecisiveness. Others over the years have become accustomed to having decisions made for them and when they are finally faced with selections by necessity, they need a period of adjustment. Most of us find that some decisions are not difficult but others confuse and upset us; we are doubtful and uncertain.

A story illustrates our frequent dilemma. A farmer was approached by a man looking for work. Taking pity on the unfortunate individual, the farmer took him to the cellar where there was a large pile of potatoes of all sizes. "Now," said the farmer, "all you have to do is put the small potatoes in that basket, the medium-sized ones over in the next basket, and the large ones in this bag. I'll be back in a couple of hours."

At the appointed time, the farmer returned, only to find the man still sitting there and the potatoes still unsorted. "What's the matter? Don't you feel well?" he asked.

"Oh, it's not that," replied the unhappy man. "I just can't make decisions!"

Some people prefer not to make their own choices. A wife, whose husband had been in the army for twenty-four years and now was a salesman, decided she would help him in his selection of clothing for each day. When he was home, she laid out the appropriate garments; when he was on the road, she included packets, each of which consisted of a folded shirt, a tie, socks, and a handkerchief all enclosed in one-gallon storage-size clear plastic bags. After his morning shower, there was everything ready for him to put on. No decisions.

How about those days when even our slightest decisions seem to be wrong! We get into the wrong line, whether it be at the gas station, the supermarket, the post office, the bank; we choose the pair of panty hose in which we discover a run just as we are going out the door with no time to change; our line at the ticket window bogs down and we miss our plane. We decide it would have been better if we had just stayed in bed.

Sometimes choices involve priority. When the late Charles Lindbergh and his wife Anne prepared to make their pioneer flight north to the Orient many years ago, one of their most burdensome tasks was deciding what to take along. Only so much weight was allowed. Each object had to be considered relative to its importance and its poundage. Piles of clothing and equipment were constantly being moved from the "going" to the "staying" groups, and the other way around.

Have you ever tried packing the possessions of a college-bound daughter into a car, especially if the college is so far away that one trip must suffice? My daughter Kathy had her clothing, stereo, chair, lamp, hair dryer, pictures, posters, and the like spread out on the floor of her room the day before we were to leave. Only a truck could possibly have taken everything. Priorities had to be established.

Some decisions involve much more drastic measures. The tale is told that centuries ago a lawgiver, Zaleucus, wrote a code of laws for the Lacrians, a tribe of people in Asia Minor. Zaleucus wanted his laws to be just and wise, and since many of the difficulties of his people were caused by drunkenness, he decreed that any man found drunk should be punished by having his eyes torn out.

Zaleucus, however, did not bargain for a decision he eventually had to make himself. The first man to be charged with drunkenness and brought before him for judgment was his own son. Zaleucus was in a quandary. Should he carry out justice as he had conceived of it, even though it meant the loss of his son's eyes, or should mercy triumph and leave the lawgiver open to the charge of favoritism, throwing the legal system into confusion? After much deliberation, Zaleucus made his decision. His son would give one eye and, in place of the other, Zaleucus would give one of his own.

Judges and juries, trying to be fair and impartial, adhering to the law and yet not forgetting the individuality of the prisoners, are faced with decisions. Doctors must decide on a course of treatment or an operation on a patient. Teachers must determine grades, some of which are subjective and dependent on their own judgment. Editors must decide what will go into newspapers and magazines. Government officials must decide on policies. The list goes on and on. The decisions are frequently not clear-cut cases of black and white, wrong or right, evil or good. Regardless of the decision, unpleasant consequences may result and one is figuratively between the devil and the deep blue sea.

The Tragedy of Indecision

Very well, we say, decisions must be made. But what if I simply cannot do so? What if I cannot get off the fence lest I make the situation even worse than it already is? What if I fear the consequences of my decision? Would it not be better to simply go along and accept whatever comes? At least then no one could blame me if things don't turn out right.

In the Bible we read, "For he who doubts is like a wave of the sea that is driven and tossed by the wind. For that person must not suppose that a double-minded man, unstable in all his ways, will receive anything from the Lord." (James 1:6-8) Or consider the passages "Choose this day . . . ." (Josh. 24:15) "How long will you go limping between two opinions?" (1 Kings 18:21)

Jules Feiffer, the cartoonist, likes to probe and poke at lives that have become too comfortable, at people who tend to procrastinate, at innate indecisiveness. In one cartoon, Feiffer depicts a man lying in a prone position with no physical activity whatever except for the movement of his jaw as he speaks:

> Pretty soon I'll have to get up.
> It's not healthy to lie here! Got to rouse myself! Got to get involved!
> Now! Right now!
> Or am I rationalizing?
> Perhaps I don't want to get up. Perhaps I feel that I have at last found my role.

> Or perhaps, though lying here attracts me, getting up
> also attracts me . . . hence my indecision . . .
> So the real issue is not getting up or lying down. The
> real issue is how honestly I feel about either move . . .
> But I must question myself relentlessly. My path is
> clear.
> I must dig!
> I must probe!
> Pretty soon I'll start probing . . .
> I'll count to three.[1]

In the King James Version of the New Testament, Peter admonishes his hearers to save themselves from an "untoward" generation. Literally, the word means *not toward*, not going forward. No decisions are made. Such a passive attitude can lead to a point where nothing matters and mere existence replaces living.

Guidelines in Decision-Making

1. One of the liveliest desk mottoes I have seen reads: *Right Now Is a Good Time*. It suggests the answer to a puzzle—just how does a good manager get all the things done for which he is responsible? How can he keep on top of his work when so many individuals are engulfed by their tasks?

One of his vice-presidents asked a busy executive when they could get together to iron out a problem that had come up. "Right now is a good time" was the immediate response. Reminded that the opinion of several other associates might be helpful, the answer was, "Fine. Right now is a good time. I'll call them in." The decision on the problem reached, the

---

1. © Jules Feiffer 1975, used by permission.

suggestion of a staff memorandum being sent out was not countered with "I'll make a note of that." No, the executive said, "Right now is a good time; ask my secretary to step in and we'll send out notifications at once."

One secret of getting things done in business or personal affairs, household duties, and other pressing activities is to do now what can be done now, postponing only those decisions which of necessity must come later.

Procrastination seems almost inherent in many persons. As parents, we are familiar with "I'll do it later" as children and young people are requested to perform certain tasks. Teachers will recognize the plea, "Can't I hand this work in a little later when I have more time?" Even adults, who certainly should be wiser, procrastinate with tasks and decisions, especially the disagreeable ones, perhaps subconsciously hoping the need for the decision will go away if ignored long enough.

We use the excuse of lack of time, but consider all the time we waste. We tend to misplace our priorities along the way and do not do the things we should, not from lack of time, but as a result of bad working habits, negative attitudes, and poor thinking. Time masters us, instead of our mastering it.

Superbusy people have found that the most can be accomplished by following a simple rule: Right now is a good time.

2. Following closely in priority is the *need to be positive.*

Lack of firmness in our decisions, even in small things, can become a great problem. The way we deal with seemingly insignificant things that come up daily—what clothing to put on, what television program to see, what theater to attend, what menu to plan—reveals something about us. Having trouble in deciding and in sticking with a decision reveals lack of inner power and strength.

A case in point is the biblical story of the temptations of Jesus in the wilderness. The tempter came to him and said, "If you are the Son of God, command these stones to become loaves of bread." Christ did not hesitate, nor did he change his decision. "Man shall not live by bread alone . . . ." Two other challenges faced him, but each time Christ made the definite decision. "You shall not tempt the Lord your God" and "You shall worship the Lord your God and him only shall you serve." (Matt. 4:1-11)

Decisions—positive decisions—must be made consistently. As parents, we find it necessary that our children have a sense of order and confidence. In our personal lives, our jobs, and our moral choices, the same holds true.

Neutrality may have its place, but inevitably comes the time when a choice must be made. In deciding a court case, the judge remains neutral while he hears the facts. But he must eventually make a decision based on those facts. Fence-straddling weakens us. Many politicians may be clever in disguising their indecisions as political expediency, but eventually, to be true to their consciences, politicians must make decisions.

A well-considered, firm decision is strength and power.

3. Times do arise when we need help in our decision-making, but we must be wary of where we seek this help. Then the decision must be made. The *Chicago Tribune* reported that Mayor Richard Daley, in explaining his modus operandi, said to a reporter from Brazil that he was the boss. "Every large business corporation or bank has a president and/or chairman of the board. He listens to various points of view. He gets advice, but in the final analysis, that leader must make the final decision."

Various considerations must be weighed, but the ultimate decision rests on the individual. Nevertheless, counsel is important for all of us. We cannot afford myriads of experts who can bring their expertise to bear on problems; therefore, we must choose our advisors carefully.

Merely talking things over with a neighbor who happens to stop by or with a friend accidentally encountered in a grocery may or may not be helpful. Such people probably give the kind of advice they feel we want to hear. Furthermore, such advice might, of necessity, be given hastily, without thinking through the matter.

An illustration comes to mind of a mother with two teen-age children and a hard-working husband. One Saturday afternoon, the man told his wife he had made an important business engagement and therefore must break a previously made date with her, to which she had been looking forward with a great deal of anticipation. In addition to the disappointment that resulted, the subject was a sore one, for she had earlier complained that his work consumed so much of his time that she might as well be a widow and her children fatherless. Annoyed, she spoke to several close friends about what had happened, and the consensus was, "Well, I wouldn't stand for it!" Neither of the close friends she consulted were known for handling their own affairs particularly adeptly. They advised that she present her husband with an ultimatum—either he spend more time with her and the family or their marriage would be in danger of breaking up.

Fortunately, before things had gone too far, this couple was brought back together through the help of their minister, who counseled them himself and also referred them to a skilled marriage counselor. The two still loved each other, and with guidance they were willing to work out their problems.

Seek out a person who himself has made a wise decision in whatever area your problem may lie. When I first moved to Montclair, one of my earliest friends was a lawyer and retired insurance executive, Ashby Bladen. Buying a house for the first time was no small undertaking for me. I asked Ashby if he would be kind enough to look over the house I had in mind and give me advice on whether or not to purchase it. One rainy day, he carefully looked over the whole structure with me, observing things I never would have noticed. At the end of the afternoon, he pronounced the house worth the money asked. He left the final decision to me, however. Throughout the years that followed, I found this friend could be relied upon for help in making various critical decisions, for he had made many wise ones for himself.

While a trusted pastor, priest, or rabbi can offer wise counsel, do not limit yourself to the clergy. Consider the reliability of the person and the background from which he draws his ideas.

4. It is well to keep in mind that the wise decision is seldom the easy one. It would indeed be foolish to anticipate approval by the majority of all, or even most, of our decisions. Mayor Richard Daley, in his conversation with the aforementioned Brazilian reporter, said, "Whether you are talking about executives of corporations, banks, and newspapers, or about public officials and leaders of political parties, someone has to make decisions. And decisions are not always popular." To prove this, I picked up my daily newspaper and counted at random ten unpopular decisions by various officials, ranging from a levy on imported crude oil, a sales tax, and an increase in property tax all the way down to a law making it illegal for a dog to defecate on a lawn without the owner having to clean it up. Decisions are not popular in all quarters.

Theologian Reinhold Niebuhr used to tell a story of an event that undoubtedly had a considerable effect on his thinking. In his Detroit pastorate he was talking with a group of boys about the Sermon on the Mount. Having expounded eloquently on the importance of turning the other cheek, he was challenged by one of the boys. The teen-ager in question was the wage earner for himself and his widowed mother through the money he earned from selling newspapers. Each day, he said, there was a fight among the newsboys to see which one would get the best corner on which to sell his papers. Was he, as a Christian, to turn the other cheek and let some other boy take the best corner and thus reduce the support he could provide for his mother and himself?

Frank Owen, an editor for a large city newspaper, and his son Paul, also an editor, for a small-town paper not far from the city where his father works, often are conscious of the risk that information they might exchange could lead to a significant story or scoop for the city daily to the detriment of the small-town paper. Therefore, the two men are careful, most of the time, not to discuss stories likely to make headlines. However, one day while visiting his father, Paul let slip an offhand remark regarding a suicide in the small town, which might have widespread implications and could lead to nationwide headlines. Frank Owen was in a quandary. As a newspaperman, he was always out in front with his headlines. On the other hand, he was aware that his son was counting heavily on this story to bring a measure of fame to his own small-town paper. Frank decided not to scoop his son.

Our decisions are not always simple ones, good over evil, right over wrong. The tragedy is that so often we must decide on the lesser of two evils rather than on an absolute good. In voting, we may find we are choosing between two mediocre individuals. We must make our decision in the light of our limited knowledge and can only hope we have done what was best under the circumstances.

When faced with a difficult decision, if we make our choice after considering the matter through prayer, we can have confidence that Christ will lead us to the best answer available. It is up to us to carry on from there.

5. Prayer does have a place in decision-making. After praying for guidance and help, we accept God's answer, which puts things in their proper perspective. Then, with the knowledge and facts we have available, we make our decision and follow our course. Great decisions are often made in the solitude of the soul. As with Jacob when he struggled with the angel at Peniel, the final outcome can be a meeting between God and man. But God will not dictate the answer; work and deliberation on man's part is essential.

INDECISION

In the familiar story of the prodigal son, the wandering son made two decisions. The first was easy. He chose to take his inheritance and embark on a life apparently full of fun and joy. His second decision was more difficult. It undoubtedly was made with a great inner struggle. The decision was to put aside his pride and go humbly back to his father's house.

Our decisions must be rooted in God's plan; then we relate that plan to the world, to our neighbor, and to ourselves.

Healing Helps

Decisions are the measure by which the character and competency of an individual can be determined. No one always makes the right choices, but here are some clues to help you on your way.

1. Give hunches a great deal of respect. An honest hunch can help you make the right decision.
2. Don't overwork yourself on easy decisions. If you set your way of life, the easy choices should come naturally.
3. Review as many facts related to your decision as you have available; study them dispassionately.
4. Try sleeping on a decision, if possible. This avoids hasty and sometimes emotional action, giving your subconscious a chance to sort things out. *Caution*: This is *not* an excuse to procrastinate.
5. Write down the pros and cons of a selection. Seeing facts in black and white may help with the final decision.
6. Make decisions with the long view in mind rather than merely the immediate effect.
7. In particular cases in which you cannot come to a decision on your own, consult a trusted counselor. Go

over the facts with him, but remember that *you* are the one to make the final decision.

8. Use the power of prayer.
9. Once the decision has been made, do not vacillate. Mulling over all those *what if*s can only lead back to indecision.

FEAR

 Courage Opens New Windows

Fear is demonstrated in a multitude of ways, some more obvious than others, some physical, some moral, some emotional. Courage, the antithesis of fear, conquers this sore spot, which is so often a source of shame to us.

A friend wrote that at last he had the opportunity to climb a mountain, something he had always wanted to do. Several friends had asked him to go along on their ascent of the third Flatiron near Boulder, Colorado.

"It was not bad," he wrote. "I had an experienced climber ahead of me. I learned, however, that reaching the summit was not the end of the experience. I had to go down as well. The descent, called rappelling, is a real exercise in trust and courage. When I first looked down, there was no down. When I looked up, I could not see my friend. There I was, hanging between up and down. I summoned up enough courage to keep me steady and learned to move slowly and to look up, as trite as that may sound."

A while ago a young French aerialist walked a tight cable stretched between the twin towers of New York City's World

Trade Center, 1,350 feet above the streets of Manhattan. In the early morning light, Philippe Petit walked and danced and glided along; he lay down on the steel cable with the assurance of a backsplasher and the grace of a matador. He exercised equal parts of ingenuity and daring in this self-expression of courage. The local authorities were not favorably impressed with this feat of daring, but nearly everyone else marveled at the courage of the young man.

Gene Tunney, the heavyweight boxer of the twenties, said, "People often ask me if I have ever been afraid. They only make me smile. One Eastern philosopher has said that any man who boasts he has never been afraid has never put out a candle with his fingers. We are all afraid. Intelligent people, those with imagination, are the ones who know the most overpowering fears, and there is only one answer to fear and that is faith. Unless we have something greater than ourselves to believe in, we are lost. We are prey to our fears unless we pray fear away."[1]

Tunney recalled that every time he stepped into the ring, he knew what fear was. One night he awakened from a sound sleep wondering what was wrong with his bed, which was shaking like a 1910 Ford. Then he realized it wasn't the bed that was shaking; he was shaking. That was the night before his fight with Jack Dempsey. Even in his dreams, Tunney was thinking about what might happen to him the next day.

What Is Courage?

If you have given the definition of courage any serious thought, you may have touched on such things as mental and moral strength, physical bravery, valor, firmness. Let's consider all of these words and the qualities they suggest and

1. *Praying Hands* © The Praying Hands Charitable Trust, 1972.

say that courage is that quality of mind that enables one to meet danger and difficulties with firmness.

In the illustrations of the mountain climber, the aerialist, and the boxer, we have seen such basic attributes of courage as trust, confidence, and the ability to face fear. We move through the ever-present problems of our daily lives, struggling to cope with them, and if we are to be successful, we need courage. These times demand something extra from us; the courage to face whatever may come lies within each of us.

In the story of *The Wizard of Oz*, Dorothy had thought lions to to be kings of the jungle, fearless, brave, willing to fight for their territory. She was amazed when she met the Cowardly Lion, who felt he lacked courage. Actually he wasn't cowardly, however; he just thought he was. The courage was there all the time, and, when called to the test, he was brave.

Frequently we think of courage as a one-shot affair. Not long ago a fire broke out in a home in a neighboring town. A passerby turned in the alarm and then returned to dash into the burning house to rescue three small children. They would have perished if this "average" person, who just happened to be going by, had not shown exemplary courage. We read of other such acts of heroism in books and newspapers. They are described on television and radio. These examples of on-the-spot courage stem from a quality that enables a person to meet sudden danger or difficulties with a strength and fortitude he did not know he possessed. It has been said that one never knows how he himself will react in an emergency situation until it occurs.

But there are other types of courage besides those that result in heroic action.

Spirit

During an interview the actress Patricia Neal recalled some tragedies that had come into her life. When her son, Theo, was three months old, his carriage was struck by a taxi running a red light on Madison Avenue. Injuries resulting from that accident necessitated years of care and a number of operations. Miss Neal's daughter Olivia died not long after. Then, while Miss Neal was bathing her other daughter, Tessa, she herself suffered a stroke. During the next hour and a half, she suffered two more strokes at the hospital.

In the interview, Miss Neal was asked, "How do you manage to retain that warm spirit and glow after all you have been through?"

Her response was that when Olivia died, religion came to mean a great deal to her, but after her series of strokes, she went through a period which is sometimes called "the dark night of the soul." The actress came out of that valley of despair and now says, "The world is fantastic. I thank God I am alive!"

In our neighborhood, among our acquaintances, or within our own families we may know persons who have that same effervescent spirit, and have it despite handicaps and problems. A woman whom I was privileged to know was dying of cancer, but even though she knew her condition, to her last breath her spirit was unquenchable and alive. She had true courage.

A mother tells of the travail suffered by the family when a teen-age daughter was killed in a schoolyard near their home. The boy next door, whose family had always been close to the girl's family, was arrested for her murder. The common response would be a desire for vengeance and a feeling of despair. Yet the family of the girl embraced the family next door with no bitterness or malice understanding their sorrow and concern as well as their own greater grief. This was courage.

Maurice Stokes, a great basketball star, was stricken with a form of encephalitis. Over 90 percent of his time had to be spent in a private room overlooking the green hills of Cincinnati. His speech was impaired. He had only minimal use of his muscles. Despite these odds, he remained a happy man, accepting each day as it came. To the surprise of those who visited him, Stokes's halting conversation was filled with quips and he laughed frequently. Those who had come to sympathize were instead inspired. This took courage.

Keeping up one's morale over a long period of time and not relaxing into despair or self-pity is an example of one meaning of courage.

Mettle

The word *mettle* suggests preparation to do one's best and implies an ingrained capacity for facing stress or strain.

In the early part of the century, an unusual advertisement appeared in the newspapers: "Men wanted for hazardous journey. Small wages, bitter cold, long months of complete darkness, constant danger, safe return doubtful. Honor and recognition in case of success."

Most persons would not consider answering such an advertisement. Yet Sir Ernest Shackleton, the Antarctic explorer, found men through this very means who were willing to sign up for Antarctic expeditions. The words proved prophetic for the brave men who volunteered. On one trip, the ship, with all supplies, was lost. The men spent twenty-one months in a living nightmare, camping on drifting ice or struggling toward civilization in three tiny boats. Yet the men who signed up not only refused to give up, they somehow also managed to remain cheerful. And they won. Every last man returned alive to civilization.

Shackleton expressed it in these words: "We faced stress. We all knew we could overcome it when challenged to do so. We pierced the veneer of outside things. We suffered, starved, and triumphed . . . we reached the naked soul of man."

We tend to try to avoid stress and strain instead of facing them head on. Perhaps pills or alcohol will make them go away, we think. We need to know more about these problems of stress and strain and their relationship to health and disease. There are many answers as yet unknown. Perhaps we dwell too much on safety, clutching our psychological security blankets and fearing to let them go. We aim for the sure thing and want things to go smoothly and not tax our ingenuity. We might fantasize dangerous and challenging situations, but they remain fantasies. We don't want to rock the boat of security, but the inability to cope with inevitable strain and stress is debilitating. In the end, we may find a world in which fewer and fewer individuals ever catch a glimpse of the raw courage of man.

If our problems are such that we cannot fight them alone, we can combine forces with others. The men on Shackleton's voyage learned to work out their problems together.

Challenge is a part of life. We are called upon at some time to face decision, stress, difficulty. Response to challenge is a part of courage.

Resolution

Resolution indicates a firmness of mind and purpose, a determination to achieve one's goal regardless of obstacles.

Robert Martin Arhelger, one of the top third-year students at Stanford Law School, showed resolution. When fall and winter approached, he showed an interest in meeting representatives of law firms who came to the campus. In the letter of introduction sent to them, he wrote, "I am slightly different from other law students you will meet. I have cerebral palsy."

Arhelger had been crippled with the disease all his life. He was unable to feed himself; he could not write. To type he had to attach a prong fastened to a band slipped over his forehead. He then would painstakingly type out the letters. Nevertheless, this young man had achieved an almost straight A average in his studies. The dean of the law school proclaimed his work "a joy to behold."

Arhelger did find a job after graduation from law school with the Federal Home Loan Bank Board. He had long before determined that his handicap would not deter him from achieving his goal. Against the advice that college was not for him, he had gone on and had consistently made the dean's list at the University of Illinois. Though his law school entrance exams were above the 90 percentile, Stanford had hesitated, but after a forty-five minute interview with an associate dean, he had been given his opportunity.

When George Washington was inaugurated as president on April 30, 1789, he stepped into a morass of troubles. In order to make the move to take over the reins of government, he was obliged to borrow 600 pounds from a friend. He found the paper money of the infant government worth next to nothing. The Union itself was near a state of anarchy. No taxes were being collected. Vermont was declaring itself an independent country; Rhode Island regarded itself as the United States, with New York, Virginia, and all the rest of the states playing the part of illegal seceders. But Washington was resolute and determined to pull the young nation together, and he did. Assembling brilliant men to work with him, in a matter of months he not only had welded the squabbling ex-colonies into a struggling but cohesive nation, but he also had established his own place in history.

Such experiences inspire us. They make us feel that we, too, can make stepping stones out of illness, trouble, difficult decisions to fulfill our own resolutions. With the right mental attitude, barricades become opportunities rather than obstacles, beginnings rather than endings. Resolution plays a part in courage.

Tenacity

In a speech at Harrow School, Winston Churchill uttered those memorable words: "Never give in! Never give in! Never, never, never. Never in anything great or small, large or petty—never give in except to convictions of honor and good sense."

Add the tenacity of such words to the resolution which we have just considered and we have a form of stubborn persistence and unwillingness to acknowledge defeat.

History is replete with heroes who exemplify tenacity. John Paul Jones, when the British demanded his surrender, uttered the now famous words, "I have not yet begun to fight," lashed his ship, the *Bonhomme Richard*, to the British *Serapis* and, in hand-to-hand combat, with sheer tenacity forced it to surrender. The battle was a milestone in American naval history. In World War II General Anthony C. McAuliffe said, "Nuts!" to the demand that he surrender, and continued to hold his beleaguered position at Bastogne.

Tenacity means holding fast, and the quality is not reserved to military contexts alone. It is found in the day-to-day living of ordinary persons. We may not win every battle, but we hang on. We have a high resolution and we cling to it. The heroism of going on is tenacity.

Ewart E. Turner, pastor of the American Church in Berlin, tells of his visit with Heinrich Niemoeller, the father of Martin Niemoeller, the outspoken cleric who had been confined to a Nazi prison camp for many months prior to the outbreak of World War II. "As we stood at the door, Grandmother Niemoeller held my left hand in her two hands. Grandfather patted my right hand. 'When you go back to America,' he said slowly, 'do not let any one pity the father and mother of Martin Niemoeller. Only pity any follower of Christ who does not know the joy that is set before those who endure the cross. Yet, it is a terrible thing to have a son in a concentration camp. Paula and I know that. But there would be something more terrible for us if God had needed a faithful martyr, and our son Martin had been unwilling.' "

Tenacity brings out the toughness in us, but it is more than the stubbornness of the fanatic. Tenacious courage has a harder and rarer aspect. It is that quality which enables us to reexamine our convictions and reject them if they do not square with the facts. Tenacity is not blindly hanging on but rather seeing clearly what we must do and then doing it despite the obstacles. In this context, tenacity combines with spirit, mettle, and resolution to form that courage which is a necessity if we are to help ourselves.

Rewards of Courage

1. *A feeling of satisfaction.* Mrs. T. Edward McCully, Jr., returned to South America to continue the work of her husband who, together with four other missionaries, had been hacked to death by the fierce Aucan tribesmen as they sought to convert the Indians to Christianity. Why did she and her children return to Ecuador? She said, "The spiritual rewards far exceed any physical discomforts or dangers."

2. *The emergence of the best that is in us.* We depend on our surface selves so much. But all the time God's mysterious, underlying strength is standing by, ready to help us. When we permit these invisible supports to buoy us up, we discover resources for healing, comfort, and power we did not realize we had. We can conquer our weaknesses.

3. *A source of joy.* In our generation we have known martyrs. Fearless witnessing for truth has brought scars to many. Yet these martyrs wear their scars, visible and invisible, with joy.

4. *A help in decision-making.* "Passing the buck" is an all too familiar exercise. Avoiding responsibility has become an art. We need to face our decisions squarely and make them as best we can. Some may not be the right ones; most of them will not make heroes of us, for we find ourselves unpopular as a result. But courage will bolster us.

5. *A closeness to God.* Many great persons in all areas of life have found that God has helped them when they needed courage and, as a result, they have felt more of a oneness with him. Trust in God has brought courage.

Healing Helps

1. Remember that courage is a quality of mind.
2. Know your purpose.
3. Be steadfast in achieving that purpose.
4. Rejoice in the freedom which courage gives you!

NONCOMMUNICATION

 The Art of Listening

At Emory University in Atlanta, Georgia, they call it "talking point." The whole idea is for the undergraduate student who is lonely and discouraged to have a place to come in to talk things over with a sympathetic listener who might have had similar problems. Charles Gershon, a medical student, said that the graduate students, many of them first-year medical students, do not intend to substitute "talking point" for psychological services when they are needed. Professional help for those with serious problems is available. A vast number of the students' difficulties stem basically from loneliness and trouble adjusting to campus life. "Most of the time," said Mr. Gershon, "all the student needs is someone to listen to him."

Not long ago a man dismissed from his job stopped in to see me. He had spent many years working for a major religious denomination. As the money crunch became tighter, fifty executives, one out of three of those employed by one agency in the denomination, had been let go. Like the heads of business corporations, the powers that be had found that overhead could by trimmed by combining or eliminating jobs.

When the evening was over, my wife asked what Jim had wanted. "I really believe he just needed someone to listen to him. He needed reassurance that another person understood him and cared about his troubles," I replied.

Such one-to-one listening is needed desperately in daily relationships, regardless of sex, age, or walk of life.

On an assignment in Louisville, Kentucky, I stopped in a restaurant for dinner. Since it was only about five o'clock, few people had yet come to eat, though several people were already sitting at the bar. In the quietness, every word spoken between bartender and his customers was audible. As I ate, I realized that the people passing their time at the bar were in search of more than a drink. The customers frequented that bar because they needed someone to hear them out, and the bartender was willing to do so. As a matter of fact, at some schools for bartenders, recommendations and suggestions for sympathetic listening are given. The desire to communicate ideas on politics, religion, and the ball team, as well as personal problems, had brought the customers to this place where they felt they could express themselves freely, and someone would listen without passing judgment.

One of the changes taking place in journalism has as its basis this matter of listening. For decades a worsening problem in journalism, the lack of opportunity for dissenting views to be seen in print, existed. Stung by charges of bias and myopia, many news executives now are finding new ways to open their pages and airwaves to the public. Various publications have overhauled their letters-to-the-editor columns, old but often neglected outlets for readers. One of the refreshing results has been that editors and publishers are actually listening to the views of their readers and acting on them.

For a long time the monthly publication for which I work has printed alongside its "Interaction" (letters-to-the-editor) feature another one called "Platform." In both features are opportunities for editors to listen to readers who wish to sound off about an issue or problem. These pages have come to be popular, with topical and intelligent interchanges of thought.

Even television has begun to listen. Stations are proclaiming, "Here we are; let's hear from you. Tell us what you have to say." More and more channels have invited rebuttals and are giving equal time to opposing sides. General news coverage has elicited comments, and complainants themselves have appeared on camera.

A popular call-in program is aired over station WIOD in Miami. The host, the Reverend John Huffman, pastor of the Key Biscayne Presbyterian Church, said, "A lot of people have some real needs which are not being met. All they want is someone to listen to them." After hearing the caller's problem, which might deal with drugs, suicide, marital difficulties, or job worries, Mr. Huffman encourages the person to whom he is speaking to think through his situation and come up with positive action. Mr. Huffman himself says little except for inserting pertinent questions or comments from time to time.

Professional psychiatrists encourage their patients to talk at great length about themselves and their problems, their hopes and aspirations. Usually the psychiatrist himself has very little to say. But he listens.

One might say that the newspaper and magazine editors, radio and television executives, ministers, and psychiatrists have something personal to gain by listening. After all, this is a part of their job. But why must we depend on professionals to do all the listening? We need not be trained in any particular field simply to listen to another express himself and to let him know that someone cares enough to spend time merely showing interest and concern.

Certainly we should listen to our loved ones, for they are the closest to us and we undoubtedly have their interests at heart. But all too often years will pass, and a person we thought we knew so well proves to be almost a stranger. But if we had been listening, we would have understood what ideas were developing, what pleas were being uttered, perhaps silently or obliquely, what needs we could have helped fulfill. One of the tough problems in family living itself is this matter of listening. Most of us need to develop a sensitivity to the persons we love.

Situation comedies and cartoons have frequently dealt with the premise that one of the marriage partners, or sometimes both, fail to listen. One cartoon shows a husband sitting in his favorite chair while his wife stands before him, hands on hips, saying, "You could at least have the common courtesy to keep quiet while we're discussing something." The line may be amusing, but it hits home for so many readers. On a television program, the hero of the story tells his girl friend that "the first thing a lady must learn to do is to listen to a gentleman." That might be so, but the gentleman should also listen to the lady.

Cultivate listening. Actually, it does not appear to be such a difficult thing to do, yet a willingness to listen and still hear the other as a separate person is a challenge to individuals who wish to stay in love or to maintain a good relationship with their families and acquaintances. Deepened sensitivity to the other individual resists the forces that tend to tune out another person.

Listening in depth is not an easy thing. The worst enemy of love and understanding is the conviction that we have already heard everything the other has to say, that we know him or her so well that all we need do is make a check mark and pass on. As soon as we begin to feel that way, we had better begin asking why, and, in a very practical manner, begin doing something about it.

A positive way to remedy the situation is to heed the instructions we used to receive at railroad crossings: STOP, LOOK, LISTEN. Here are some helps in becoming a good listener.

Stop

One of the obvious places to begin practicing the art of listening is restraining our impulse to interrupt. For example, since I travel extensively in the course of my work, I often find myself cutting in on conversations in which travel is the subject. As the person describes his visit to India, I cannot resist asking, "Did you get to the Taj Mahal?"

"No," comes the somewhat apologetic reply, "we just didn't have the time, but . . ."

"You missed a great sight. The Taj Mahal is the most outstanding . . ." and on and on.

There is no particular reason why I should interrupt with information to top that of my conversant. Having been in that position myself I know that what it amounts to is a put-down, leading to annoyance and frustration.

In the summer of 1974, I conducted a tour of Alaska for thirty-seven persons. One of the group became absolutely obnoxious with her constant interruptions at the table or even in conversations which did not concern her at all. It appeared there was no place she had not visited, no subject on which she was not an expert, no problem she could not solve, or no prominent person she did not know. In addition, she knew how to do everything better than anyone else. In the long run, her nonlistening proved to be a unifying factor for the group. In avoiding her, we seemed to develop a spirit of comradeship and made a genuine attempt to listen to each other.

Name-dropping and listing of accomplishments could reveal that we ourselves are not secure. Certainly we cannot have helpful relationships with others when we are so engulfed by our own interests that we have little time for the needs of our companions. We are quick to speak and slow to listen, anxious to impress and fearful of demands.

The next time we are tempted to show we have remarkable knowledge about a subject, let's stop and think. If we give the other person a chance, we might even learn something we did not know. Surely we will be strengthening the sense of communication in the other person.

Look

St. Paul, writing to the Philippians, said, "Do nothing from selfishness or conceit, but in humility count others better than yourselves. Let each of you look not only to his own interests, but also to the interests of others." (Phil. 2:3, 4) These words hit us right where we are living, and we can realize our shortcomings. Paul is saying, "Fix your attention upon others." We are to consider our neighbors and not always ourselves.

If we look seriously at another person, we will find out things which may help us understand a situation and have said of us, "He really knows my needs and cares profoundly."

At work one day, a co-worker passed me in the hallway on a day when I was not feeling well. He rhetorically asked, "How are you?" I don't customarily complain about illness or problems, but on this particular day, I would not have minded discussing my feelings. Instead of stopping and really looking at me, though, my friend hurried past before I had an opportunity to say anything to him.

How often have we been guilty of this same thoughtlessness? We ask a friend, "How are things going with you?" But we show that we actually could not care less. However, this might be just the moment that the friend needs to discuss a disturbing situation and instead of rushing on we could help him by stopping and expressing interest.

There is nothing wrong with healthy self-concern, but too

often we are the ones doing the talking and not the looking, not listening. Upon later reflection, I thought that perhaps my friend had serious stresses in his life that blinded him to problems of others. Perhaps I needed to be the one offering the opportunity to communicate. We both were wrapped up in our own concerns and oblivious to problems of others.

At a meeting with a group of denominational leaders, I anticipated a time of mutual concern and encouragement. But everyone around the table seemed bent on impressing the others. Each mentioned his own most recent accomplishments. One person interrupted another, always being one step ahead. Where was the looking and listening? Each was impatient to get the spotlight. I, too, was guilty, for I wanted to add my boasting lest no one would give me proper recognition. But as I walked away from the room after the meeting, I kept asking myself, "Why can't we really look at each other? Why can't we be patient and await the other person's expression?" After people have been with us, do they go away impressed with how great *we* are or how great *they* can be?

When listening, look directly into the eyes of the speaker. Eyes reveal sincerity or insincerity. If you are perceptive, you can learn much more about that individual than his words will tell you. Are you self-conscious about looking a person in the eye, having to make an effort to confront people squarely?

Listen (*Really* Listen)

A friend of mine found himself in a physical and mental quandary. A single-minded man, he had driven himself hard for many years, wanting his children, his wife, his parents to be proud of him. He made his life a constant drive toward what he considered success. One day a sharp pain in his chest presaged a serious heart condition. Fortunately, he survived the first attack. After several weeks in the hospital, he learned he would have to forgo his old pace if he wished to live much longer. Gloomily, he accepted the prescribed rest and slowdown.

Going up to New Hampshire for several weeks, he found himself in a quiet, wooded area where a new world opened before him. In that setting he learned something; he learned to listen, really listen. In the hectic rush and press of modern living he had forgotten how. While he was recuperating, my friend learned the hard way to put his own drives and wishes in the background and to understand other people.

Merely being present physically does not ensure listening. We must comprehend the words and the thoughts behind the words, the thoughts behind the actions. Surface listening is not enough. An in-depth awareness can tell us when another person is trying to communicate something even when he might not fully understand it himself. The empathy of identifying with the speaker is "walking awhile in the other man's moccasins."

We all have had the experience of trying to converse with someone who mows us down like a power mower with his views, never hearing what we might have to say. After a while, we tend to tune him out. When someone speaks to you, try to listen carefully. When he pauses and you are tempted to change the subject, remember that unless what you are about to say is based on what he has just said to you, your words will be worthless to him. Try to quell that impulse to interject *your* ailments, *your* experiences, or even *your* advice. Hear him out first, and be careful with dispensing that advice. You can do a great service to someone by helping share the burden of his problems simply through your presence and close attention.

Learning to listen is an art with healing powers.

Healing Helps

Let the old, familiar railroad crossbar warning speak a friendly message to your needs:

STOP

interrupting conversation
avoiding hearing other out
bragging about your own accomplishments

LOOK

at the interests of others
right into the eye of those you face
deeper and gain understanding

LISTEN

for the opportunities to help others
for a chance to show love and concern

THEN

by obeying the rules
to stop, look, and really listen
you can heal others.

GUILT

7 *The Overwhelming Burden*

Sue has just told her mother she was at the library until closing time working on her report for history. Her mother nods, accepting this, for she has no reason to doubt Sue. She had indeed gone to the library, but not to work on her report. She went to meet Tom, of whom she was well aware her parents disapproved, and after half an hour of perfunctorily looking through the card catalog, they left and went for a long walk. Sue will complete her report, no one will say anything to her mother about the contradiction in time spent at the library, but Sue feels uneasy.

George has brought flowers home to Marge and she's delighted. Since her bridge club meets at her house tomorrow, she carefully arranges the carnations in the cut-glass vase. She kisses George an extra time for being so thoughtful. George, however, doesn't feel too happy and says little the rest of the evening. After all, why mention he took his miniskirted new secretary out for lunch today?

Bill has received an A on a crucial test. Now he'll be on the honor roll and the college of his choice will be more impressed with his grades. However, he doesn't even mention the test at home. He might have received the A even if he hadn't seen a copy of the test the night before it was given, strictly by accident, of course.

Mary, after considering various alternatives, has decided to place her aged mother in a nursing home where she will receive the best of care, better than Mary can give her any longer. Mary has given much thought to this decision and truly feels it is for the best, but she is unhappy just the same.

What do Sue, George, Bill, and Mary have in common? A sense of guilt, regardless of reason or degree. Their actions all can be rationalized, and they have used this approach. Eventually, they even may forget just why they feel guilty. Their lives probably will not be affected drastically, yet at this particular time they are aware of guilt feelings, feelings which may or may not surface in other guises in later years.

Guilt is one emotion man shares with no other animal on our planet. He alone can have a painful feeling of self-reproach resulting from the belief he has done something wrong or immoral. Yet guilt is not an innate feeling; we *learn* guilt from various sources. As individuals we feel guilt in many degrees and for different reasons. As a matter of fact, psychologists tell us that some guilt feelings can be good, resulting in the beginning of new energy for better things.

Guilt can be both conscious and subconscious. We may not know exactly why we feel uncomfortable and ill at ease with ourselves, but we are sensitive to this bothersome emotion, one which may even lead us to do strange and possibly harmful things.

As we consider the various causes and symptoms of guilt, we will better understand ourselves and our personal reactions to situations. And as our understanding increases, we can rid ourselves of nagging twinges of self-reproach, adjust our lives to accommodate them, or use them to lead better lives.

Roots of Guilt

On the April 28, 1975, program on Channel 13, an educational TV station, one of a series, titled "The Thin Edge," devoted the entire time to a discussion of guilt—its causes, its results, and suggestions for its alleviation. The psychologists and psychiatrists mentioned parents and childhood experiences, religious training, and peer group pressures as being the basic influences. Over the years we "learn" our guilt feelings, sometimes in later years not even recalling their sources.

1. *Parents and childhood experiences.* In childhood, certain rules of conduct are set up by families. For example, in my wife's case she was not permitted to play cards, attend movies, or sew on Sunday since this was a day for rest and meditation. To this day, she has uneasy feelings when she does such things. She no longer sees these narrow restrictions as rules of morality, but still the guilt feeling, however faint, remains. In my own case, whether or not to attend church on Sunday was never in question. Barring grave illness, Sunday found one in church. Now on the Sundays I miss church attendance, for whatever reason, I find a letdown which exists throughout the rest of the week, a feeling that something is wrong.

Parents scold children for various acts—spilling the milk, not responding to toilet training, crossing the street unattended, breaking a dish, striking a brother or sister—the list is legion. Guilt feelings result, some for the protection and betterment of the child, others to trouble and haunt for years to come.

Paul Tournier, in his book *Guilt and Grace*, points out that upbringing is a sense of guilt on an intensive scale. Concerned about their children and their success, most parents do a great deal of scolding; even discreet and silent reprobation suggests a feeling of guilt: "Aren't you ashamed to behave like that?"[1]

Basically, children wish to live up to the expectations of their parents, to receive their commendation; they may go to extremes to achieve it. Frequently, the child misinterprets or misunderstands what is expected of him, but, unless the situation is cleared up, he can go on into his adult life with unfulfilled expectations dogging him. He cannot or does not consciously want to do those things he feels he ought to do, and guilt results. How deeply this will affect him depends on a variety of other circumstances.

Johnny is caught "playing doctor" with a neighbor child; his curiosity about the opposite sex has led him to investigate that which he suspects might be frowned on by his mother. On discovery, he no longer suspects; he knows to his sorrow how she feels about his actions. Severe punishment results so that he "will not do it again." Perhaps Tommy or Mary, in investigating their own bodies, discover that masturbation results in a good feeling. Their parents, however, let them know in no uncertain terms that "nice people don't do that—only nasty, perverted people."

Later in life Johnny, Tommy, and Mary may find themselves caught up in various sexual hang-ups, and they are unable to enjoy normal sexual relations with their mates. They don't know why, for those childhood incidents have been forgotten. But the guilt remains.

Jean, a quick-tempered child, has endured spankings and banishment to her room for venting her anger both vocally and physically. As she grows older, she learns to control those impulses, at least on the surface, and is known for her calm demeanor. But Jean knows how angry she really is and feels guilty because of it.

1. Paul Tournier, *Guilt and Grace* (New York: Harper, 1962).

Wilma, when she was eight years old, stole a box of crayons from a nearby store. She was not apprehended, and her mother never noticed she had them. But Wilma felt guilty nevertheless; but she never returned the crayons. That guilt over an inexpensive box of crayons has remained with her over the years.

Certainly no one would claim that all these examples of guilt stemming from childhood experiences will result in damaging complexes, but there are enough cases in which they do for us to consider them as we attempt to heal our sore spots of guilt.

2. *Religion.* According to Harvey Cox, professor of religion at Harvard Divinity School, religion has long placed an overemphasis on guilt and through this stress has sought to become more of a force in people's lives. Most church rituals include some confession of guilt. We may read: "We have left undone those things which we ought to have done; we have done those things which we ought not to have done." Through the church, we seek atonement for sin, both personal and corporate. The Roman Catholic Church uses the individual confession of sins to a priest, with penance to follow. Even without individually assigned penance, we often punish ourselves in one way or another for the religious rules we have broken or not lived up to.

The Victorian age, with its overemphasis on sexual guilt and stress on proper public behavior, has done much to influence more of our present-day religious thinking than we might care to admit. The movement away from Victorian demands has brought with it all sorts of guilt feeling which we try to intellectualize away.

By means of articles, sermons, lectures, and discussion groups, we probe and delve into commandments, duties, and laws, sometimes reading into these basically good ideas much more than was originally meant to be there. And we tend to feel guilt, for who among us is perfect?

GUILT

We are ashamed of not feeling more compassion when we view pictures of the atrocities of war or hear heartrending personal case histories of people in need. We feel guilt because we are unable to suffer, even vicariously, with these people.

The Ten Commandments, the words of Jesus, additional religious rules and regulations of many religious groups surround us and, since we cannot possibly live up to these ideals at all times, we reproach ourselves. Unless we are unbearably self-righteous, we must admit that there are times when we do not tell the exact truth; when we speak ill of another; when we do not play the Good Samaritan because we are suspicious of the "man lying by the side of the road"; when we are envious or covetous; to say nothing of the more obvious and flagrant departures from a "good" religious life.

Even those who no longer profess a religious belief are influenced to a degree by deep-rooted ideas. In their very protestations, they, as did the queen of the play within a play in *Hamlet*, "protest too much."

Throughout man's history, his feeling of guilt at the breaking of some religious law or tenet has led him to try to expiate his sin.

3. *Peer group.* In addition to parental and childhood influences and our religious upbringing, our peer group and the general expectations of society add to our burden of guilt.

Bill and three of his friends and their dates have gone out to have something to eat after the school play. The "something to eat" turns out to be a drinking and necking party. Bill actually has little desire to drink. As a matter of fact, his childhood training has presented it as an evil habit. And though little has been said about it at home, he is sure the necking party would also be frowned on. Yet he does not want to be a spoilsport or a prude, and he does want to be included in later social affairs. His parents trust him and will not be waiting up for him, so he really does not fear their discovering what he's done. He goes along with the gang, but he's uncomfortable.

Charles knows who has been vandalizing some of the empty houses in the next block. But when authorities ask for information regarding the culprits, Charles remains silent. He doesn't want to be a "stool pigeon" or a "squealer." He doesn't feel right about it, though.

Polly fails to go to the Junior Red Cross meeting with her friends as she has promised. She has no interest in making favors for the party the group is giving for disadvantaged children and instead has gone home to listen to some new records. The next day she feels ill at ease with her friends as they talk about the meeting.

As we grow older, we find there are certain things expected of us which we either cannot or will not do. Most people in our society are imbued with the idea of monetary success in life, or at least in going up the social or educational ladder. But when we reach a certain age, we realize the chances are slim that we will fulfill those expectations. We are not pleased with ourselves as a result.

Ralph began his career as a salesman with every intention of working his way to the top, Horatio Alger style. Somehow, success has eluded him, and at forty-five he is still a salesman, and a mediocre one at that. He knows moments of panic, interspersed with those of guilt. His family, his friends, he himself had anticipated his success. He has failed.

Louise always looked forward to a stage career in which she would be a star, receiving the adulation of thousands. Now she is in her middle years and has had only a few minor successes to her credit. In the past five years she has had only an occasional, unimportant part to play. She not only feels discouraged, she feels guilty. She had fully expected to be a star and felt others expected it of her as well.

Psychologists tell us that individuals, usually men, in their forties and fifties suddenly come to the realization that this is as far as they will go on the way to success. Such realization can be a blow, resulting in all sorts of problems.

In our mobile society, the older generation frequently finds itself in homes for the aged, retirement homes, and nursing homes, rather than in the bosom of their families. Such an arrangement may be the most practical way or even the only way; the older people themselves may prefer it that way. Nevertheless, regardless of explanations, guilt feelings surface as far as the children and grandchildren are concerned. After all, in a sense they are casting these older folk aside after all they have done. Does not the family owe something to its members? Somehow, a feeling of ingratitude lingers. Rationalization, in the form of repeated explanations, does not help.

A problem often faced by families of loved ones who are afflicted with a terminal illness, incapacitation because of an accident, or mental retardation is one of self-reproach. "What did I do that such a thing could happen to my loved one? It must be my fault. But what did I do?" Somewhere along the line has grown the feeling that the good person and his family are rewarded and the bad person is punished, even to the later generations. Anguished parents have been caught in the vicious cycle of blaming themselves, each other, or even God when they learn their child will not be normal. Thus they are burdened with a devastating sense of guilt which can destroy what security they do have.

Conversely, some persons feel they are prospering or are the recipients of good fortune while others far more worthy are suffering or dying. As Archie Bunker laments, "No matter how good the little sheep are, they still become lamb chops." No logical explanation of the luck of some and the misfortune of others is apparent, and guilt results. Survivors of the concentration camps have commented on this guilt feeling—why did they survive while others, perhaps members of their own family, did not? Frequently their guilt feelings are stronger than those of the persons who perpetrated the atrocities. Somehow, in a way they cannot understand, they have cheated someone.

Inherent beliefs and ideas of man are not completely changed in a generation. Therefore, it is not only the pressure of our peer groups or society today but also past ideas and customs which influence our thinking, our actions, our guilt.

4. *Symptoms*. The symptoms of guilt are as varied and complex as the individuals involved. When these symptoms lead beyond the vague self-reproach feelings or when the individual is no longer able to squarely face himself to work out his own answers, professional help is needed.

There may be a tendency to withdraw from society. On the other hand, some individuals seem determined to discuss the situation over and over, as if seeking agreement for their action. Over the telling, facts become embellished with more details.

A change in personality may be noted. Occasionally, a person may suddenly break out in a rash of good deeds for everyone, a sort of public penance for an unconfessed guilt. Actual physical illness can result, as if the resultant sympathy from others could somehow erase the dissatisfaction within oneself.

In a more extreme way, the guilty person attempts to literally "block out" whatever it was he did, and he succeeds in pushing the memory back into his subconscious where it tends to do more damage than if he had faced up to it in the first place. Studies indicate an alarming number of single-car accidents which appear to be deliberate, as if the person involved wanted to die because of hidden or overwhelming guilt feelings.

Coping with Guilt

Before attempting to cope with our own guilt feelings, whatever they may be, we should realize that guilt is common to all persons in one degree or another. Such feelings fluctuate widely, depending on backgrounds, experiences, individual temperaments, and social milieu. The realization that we are not strange or different should give us some reassurance that we can begin to face our specific guilts.

Paul Tournier in *Guilt and Grace* says: "Daily guilt is of much interest to the doctor and the psychologist for it is linked with relationship to others, with criticism by others, with social scorn and with feelings of inferiority. Remorse, bad conscience, shame, embarrassment, uneasiness, confusion, shyness, even modesty: there is a link between all of these."[2]

Guilt has positive aspects. Without a sense of guilt, we would lack conscience. In one sense, the feeling of self-reproach is a danger signal, a warning we should heed, a deterrent to thoughts or actions which might be harmful or immoral. We can also look upon the stirrings of guilt as a starting point in bettering our lives, expanding our humanity. So, while on the one hand guilt feelings inhibit, on the other they may serve to free us from past errors or contemplated ones.

Guilt may indicate a problem that we are compelled to face. If, after a sincere effort on our own part, we still cannot reach the basis of the difficulty, we should not hesitate to turn to a competent psychiatrist for help. At one time, a certain stigma was attached to psychiatric treatment, but such is not the case any longer. The treatment usually is expensive, it is true, but if the problem is severe enough to adversely affect our lives and our relationships with others, the money would be well spent.

Sometimes group therapy, again under competent and qualified leadership, may be the answer. Through discussion and role-playing, guilt feelings long hidden may be brought to the surface and confronted and dealt with in a positive manner. The emphasis here is on *competent* leadership.

We ourselves can do a great deal toward understanding our own feelings and finding the reasons we feel as we do toward certain things. If we are aware, or make ourselves aware, of our reactions, we have taken the first step. One way to become aware is to make a written list. Too easy? It is amazing how transferring our guilt into the written word and then reading over the list can give us a more objective perspective from which to view our problems. We want to deal with causes, not merely symptoms, but after reviewing our lists, we may perceive a pattern which will help us.

If possible, make amends, correcting the situation even if it takes a great deal of willpower and may result in some sort of punishment. For example, if we feel a sense of guilt for neglect of duties or the padding of an expense account, we can begin at once to fulfill or even surpass what is expected of us at work. We can keep a scrupulously accurate record of our expenses, even if we formerly rationalized the padding by claiming our salary was too low anyhow. If we feel we really should have sent those letters or cards to relatives, shut-ins, and friends, we can take immediate action by doing so, despite the old excuse that we are too busy right at the moment.

Where such a simple solution is not possible, consider alternate ideas to remedy the situation. These might involve changing our life-style, or at least the part of it causing the guilt feeling. This, of course, is more easily said than done, for it may result in financial losses or alienation of friends. Such a course needs to be carefully considered before we embark upon it. It is one thing to make a resolution and quite another to live up to it.

Confession frequently alleviates the feeling of guilt, but unless that confession is followed by a program of action or change, the guilt returns. We must also consider the pain which might be visited on someone else in the process. For example, confessing to a spouse that one has been unfaithful in the past but never will be again in the future might give that person a respite from a nagging guilt, but it also might result in a deterioration in the marriage, especially if the spouse is not of a forgiving nature.

Psychiatrists tell us that while a person may seek forgiveness from others, he may be unable to forgive himself, carrying the burden despite expressions of forgiveness from others. Somehow even reassurances compound the guilt feeling. Paradoxically, self-forgiveness is a most difficult state to achieve.

In the consideration of coping with guilt feelings, the most important realization should be that, regardless of the complexity of our emotions, God understands us much more than we understand ourselves. He does not need explanations, excuses, rationalizations. He can make a complete restoration of our emotional well-being if we turn to him with our burden of self-guilt. We need no tricks or gimmicks. What we do need is a willingness to admit our guilt, our shortcomings, our wrong actions to him. And we need to be willing to accept forgiveness from him.

If we cannot do those most difficult things—forgive ourselves and accept God's forgiveness—all the public confessions and good deeds in the world will not help rid us of our guilt.

If we find the problem of our guilt compounding itself, we may need to use professional help to discover what lies behind our self-reproach and to accept ourselves once more as children of God.

Healing Helps

1. Accept the fact that guilt is a feeling shared by all.
2. See if dealing with guilt feelings can work for your benefit.
3. Make a list of the things about which you feel guilty. Be specific.
4. Make amends where possible.
5. Make a conscious attempt to change your life-style as it relates to these feelings.
6. Be willing to accept professional help if you cannot deal with your guilt on your own.
7. Forgive yourself.
8. Accept God's forgiveness.

ANXIETY

The Rust of Life

The very word *anxiety* carries with it a concern for the future, but it is an uneasy concern, distressed and apprehensive. The interesting corollary to the definition is that, since the future deals with what is yet to be, these anxieties causing us so much unhappiness may not even come to pass. Be that as it may, anxiety, especially acute conditions of it, has caused more psychological havoc than have most of our other sore spots. It can have physical, emotional, and mental repercussions.

To merely state that an individual should not be acutely anxious is not enough. To one so afflicted, such words mean nothing. What that person needs is an opportunity or way to deal with his problem. He needs encouragement and a practical means of determining which are needless worries and which are the ones requiring action. He wants a clear outlook, a perspective from which he can more accurately judge his feelings.

The universality of worry and anxiety is borne out by the fact that the famous insurance company, Lloyds of London, has made a fortune on people's tendencies to worry about things that will probably never happen.

One woman of an orderly nature realized that worry and anxiety were ruining her life and deliberately took a period of time to tabulate and consider those worries that plagued her. She came up with the following information:

Forty percent never happened.

Thirty percent involved decisions or actions which could not have been altered, regardless of her anxiety.

Twelve percent came from criticism, mostly untrue, by others who felt inferior to her.

Ten percent dealt with her health, which, unless she consulted a physician for treatment, only worsened due to her anxiety.

Eight percent were legitimate worries dealing with problems she must face in life.

Worry and anxiety in themselves are destructive, the only possible good resulting from positive action brought to bear on situations coming under the 8 percent category mentioned above.

This chapter will discuss the various aspects and types of anxieties which beset us, with mention of results of which we must be aware. The main thrust of the chapter, however, will be to give help in dealing with the problems and eliminating or at least alleviating the most damaging.

Aspects

A physician, speaking from long experience, warns us that the person who assumes undue importance of the common-place incidents, taking personally the gossip of idle speakers, the chance statement of a superior at work, the possibility of future disaster, is courting physical illness.

ANXIETY

Anxiety in itself does not solve problems and only tends to lead to mental, emotional, and physical deterioration. In nine cases out of ten, breakdowns occur, not because of overwork, but because of worry or anxiety.

Fatigue is a direct result of anxiety, even more than the hours of actual labor involved. Physical fatigue resulting from strenuous use of the muscles is temporary, but mental and emotional fatigue saps our bodies of energy-giving forces for long periods of time. Unless dealt with firmly and decisively, anxieties can place us on the treadmill of worry, fatigue, lack of productive work, more worry, more anxiety.

Hugh Blair has said, "Anxiety is the poison of human life." Not only are our physical bodies impaired but so are our reactions to other facets of human existence. Overriding anxiety pushes other thoughts, other persons into the background. We are unable to concentrate productively or calmly, we cannot concern ourselves with friends and family, we fail to take action. The end result is that the sorrows of tomorrow are not alleviated or healed and today is robbed of its strength and possibilities. We might compare our state of mind to a fog surrounding us.

In days of general economic uncertainty, anxiety becomes particularly noticeable, though this is by no means the only time it manifests itself. Students are anxious about the possibility of obtaining jobs in their chosen fields, or in any field. In the case of Joe, a college senior, the problem assumed such proportions that he could no longer concentrate on his final semester's work. Discouraged by negative responses to his tentative job inquiries and overwhelmed by the statistics he had read in the newspapers, he became withdrawn. He refused to pursue suggested avenues of employment, yet thought constantly about the fact that in less than three months he would be among the unemployed.

Men with families have also joined the ranks of the unemployed. Through no fault of their own, they have been laid off because of the economic crunch, some despite years of seniority. Many have given up entirely and no longer even attempt to find work. Articles and books have been published dealing with the anxieties brought on by these and similar circumstances.

The mother of young friends of ours is consumed by anxiety whenever they travel any distance from home, whether by car, plane, or ship. She is certain some terrible accident will either injure or kill them. As a matter of fact, she begins her anxiety attacks even before they leave. No amount of reassurance does any good, and she is literally sick with anxiety. Her family is affected adversely by her emotions, and unless she conquers her overconcern she will not be the only family member with psychological problems.

Young people sometimes are anxious about their future social life. What if no one asks them to the prom? What if they ask someone and are refused? What if all their friends have dates for the beach picnic and they do not? What if their attire is entirely unsuitable for whatever occasion they are to attend?

People of varying ages are found to be anxious about their future health. How can they assure themselves longevity? How can they guarantee absence of pain and disease? After reading the newspapers they fear accidents and attacks. Their anxieties literally make them prisoners, and they tend to fall prey to quacks and promotors of various gimmicks.

Anxiety about the future faces many who have gone through a grief experience, especially widows and widowers. In a psychiatric study it was found that most research subjects during the first year of bereavement feared a nervous break-down, an inability to cope with financial problems, or acceptance of reality. Fortunately, a follow-up study showed that for the most part these anxieties were groundless and that they could cope with life.

A common anxiety is over what others think of us. We may be obsessed with the idea that our friends and acquaintances will ridicule our appearance, our actions, our associates. We may feel that as a result of their ridicule our future will be uncertain. Our concern over what *might* happen blunts our recognition of the right thing to do, the proper course of action to take.

Dealing with Anxiety

Plato said that nothing in the affairs of men is worthy of great anxiety. We are assured in the Bible that no man can add one cubit to his stature by worrying. The motto of a detective in the New York Bomb Squad reads, "Worry is worse than trouble—the worst never happens." And yet people do worry.

The source of the basic anxieties in human nature is a feeling of being alone and helpless in a hostile world. We have our private anxieties; one cannot state firmly, "I will no longer be anxious about anything," and live within that resolution for long. However, we need not permit these incipient worries for the future to control us. Instead, we can take steps to control them. *Concern* for the future is one thing, for it leads us to make plans, to live an ordered life, to be active. However, overanxiety is entirely different, for it is counterproductive, putting an unbearable burden on our minds and bodies.

Our mental attitude needs to be one of action, self-discipline. We can take only one step at a time. A physician remarked to a worried patient, "You will never be here longer than one day at a time." Like our friend who sat down to determine what her worries were like by percentages, we can take the first step by writing specifically what we are anxious about. Is it the future of our children, our own future, the value of our real estate, the success of a coming dinner or party, the opinion of friends and acquaintances, our job, the nation's future? The list, of course, depends on the individual. Think of all the things you worry over, large or small, trivial or important. Such listing should be done over a period of a week or so, with the idea that we are noting not only the things which first occur to us.

Since the basic idea is to deal with solutions instead of problems, reread the list after a period of still a few more days and from the perspective of even this reasonably short time, you can approach your solutions more objectively.

After crossing out the anxieties which no longer exist (for there will be some of these), try to be honest enough to determine which of those still on the list will undoubtedly never happen. Life being what it is, no one can speak with absolute certainty in this regard, but surely common sense can be a guide.

Next, consider the events which could not be changed, no matter how much you worried. Can anxieties in themselves prevent air accidents, car collisions, the length of life?

How about those worries caused by criticism by others? Will anxiety really make any difference to those people? Will it change their minds? Are they by their very criticism showing their own basic feeling of inferiority by trying to pull us down to their level?

Unanalyzed health problems certainly cannot be cured by anxiety. Anxiety does not help the analyzed problems, either, and may even worsen the condition. Simply *fearing* the worst can in no way alleviate it.

Now for the action part as we seek to *do* something to relieve our legitimate anxieties, the 8 percent we can do something about.

If health is the problem, consult doctors, a number of doctors if necessary. Do as they recommend with the optimistic view in mind that the treatment can help. If the problem proves to be a truly serious one, acceptance of its presence will bring more ease of mind than all the worries in the world. For some time, an acquaintance had been worrying over certain physical symptoms. His wide reading only concerned him the more. He knew something must be wrong, but what? For several months he refused to see a physician, fearing the diagnosis. When he finally did consult his family doctor he was referred to a specialist who spelled out the problem very clearly to him. He was indeed seriously ill and a cure could not be promised. But once he found out what was wrong and could take steps to combat it with the best of scientific treatment, it was as if a great burden had been lifted from his mind.

Financial difficulties certainly can lead to anxiety regarding the future, but instead of wringing your hands and bemoaning the turn of fate, formulate a plan of some sort. The plan may change as conditions change, but at least a program of action is there.

Consider what capabilities you have in another line of work. An automobile salesman, caught in his agency's cutback, was unable to find another position in selling and marketing. As he was lamenting this fact to a friend, she reminded him of the excellent photographic work he had done for her at her daughter's wedding. For years, photography had been a hobby, and he not only took excellent pictures but also developed them to bring out their best qualities. Free-lance photography, beginning among friends and acquaintances in his home town, proved to be the door to a source of income. Another friend, handy in woodworking, took on minor carpentry jobs for friends, and eventually this led to an entirely new type of work which he enjoyed much more than his previous job. Writing is still another way of utilizing skills heretofore used only as relaxation.

How about economizing? In noting in detail actual purchases, we are amazed at the number of nonessential or even duplicating items we buy. While careful economizing will not bring in extra cash, it certainly will cut down on the amount of money needed. A word of caution should be added here. The frame of mind in which the economizing is done is important. If the family or individual approaches the cutbacks in a spirit of cooperation and challenge rather than one of incrimination and self-sacrifice, the whole exercise helps not only the finances but the morale as well. But if bitterness, inequity, and argument are entailed, then additional problems are added to an already bad situation.

Much has been written lately about skill-bartering, practiced generations ago with great success and now offered as an aid, not only to the financial picture, but also to the morale. For example, a person handy with tools, in sewing, in cooking, or the like can certainly exchange products or labor with someone who can instruct in music, art, dancing, drama, or intellectual pursuits. Skill-bartering has been done on an individual or family basis with great ingenuity shown as to the skills exchanged. With thought, we can come up with our own ideas on relieving the financial crunch, and in the process, the anxiety lessens or disappears entirely.

Perhaps anxiety over one's personality or appearance is the problem. Again, take positive action. What are your strong or positive points? Under the guise of false modesty or timidity, many individuals find only fault with themselves. The realization of outstanding qualities leads to a higher self-opinion. Observe the nervous habits of others, then check to see if you yourself might be unconsciously biting your nails, scratching your head or ear, blinking your eyes rapidly, or failing to look the other person in the eye. If you are, make an effort to correct these and other similar habits.

If one is inclined to anxiety because of a negative feeling about his personality, he should keep well informed so that he can converse intelligently, or listen intelligently. If he feels concerned that his conversation, however knowledgeable, does not come across well, he should practice describing things of interest—if possible taping descriptions and comment, then playing back the tapes. This is a method my speech teacher in college used. At first, I was appalled to hear my voice; it was not as I imagined it at all. But by practice, speaking more slowly and distinctly, using emphasis, not dropping my voice at the end of each sentence, I gradually improved and eventually was able to speak before congregations and other audiences effectively. I had to learn to assess myself as objectively as possible, sometimes a painful process, and then seek to improve myself. My anxiety about speaking gradually lessened.

Still another way to deal with anxiety is to pretend, for the moment, that the concern for the future should indeed come to pass. Exactly what should be done? What measures are to be taken? In the visualization, the anxiety is taken out of the dark realm of the unknown and is brought into the light to action, thus minimizing the fear involved.

Mrs. Rosa Jones of Syracuse, New York, when asked the secret of her long life at 102, gave this advice: "Go to bed early, get plenty of rest, and just don't worry about anything. Do just as little worrying as you possibly can."

The Bible tells us, "Therefore do not be anxious about tomorrow, for tomorrow will be anxious for itself." (Matt. 6:34) The power of God is not limited. Trust him to help take care of whatever may be ahead, and live constructively in the present.

Healing Helps

1. List as many anxieties as trouble you in any way.
2. With a period of time to aid in getting your perspective straight, evaluate these anxieties.
3. Decide which anxieties may prove to be valid ones, ones which require action.
4. Take a definite course of action to alleviate or, if possible, eliminate these anxieties.

5. Be willing to change your life, if necessary, in order to implement this action.
6. Keep in mind that you can trust God always. Regardless of what the future will bring, he is with you to support you and give you the strength you will need.

REGRET

Stumbling Block
or Stepping-Stone

The line of the poet John Greenleaf Whittier in the poem "Maud Muller," which reads:

> For of all sad words of tongue or pen,
> The saddest are these: "It might have been!"[1]

epitomizes the sore spot of regret. Whereas anxiety projects worry about what is to come in the future or even what the future results of past actions might be, regret looks backward.

Only an immature person claims never to have done anything he is sorry for or regrets, for we are all prone to mistakes in action and judgment, but to spend the present in useless, backward glances is self-defeating. True, we learn from the past to avoid mistakes in the present and future, but Prochnow was right when he said, "Forget the past. No one becomes successful in the past."

1. John Greenleaf Whittier, "Maud Muller," in *The Silver Treasury of Light Verse*, Oscar Williams, ed. (New York: New American Library, Mentor Books, 1957).

Unfortunately, it is not easy to forget what one desires to cast from his mind. It is as if he is told to stop thinking of green spiders. Immediately, his mind dwells upon green spiders. Some memories we wish to keep, and it is wise to recall mistakes which can be remedied. Regret, however, has the connotation of sorrow, a wish we could change certain past events or actions.

In this chapter we will consider the futility of regret and suggest steps to be taken in dealing with haunting and harmful thoughts of past occurrences.

The Futility of Regret

A middle-aged man broke the self-imposed wall of reserve he had erected around himself when he came to me for advice concerning his frequent spells of depression. After I had listened for some time to his tale of woe which involved his feeling that he was not socially accepted in circles he desired to associate with, despite his success in the business world, he made a revealing statement. He said, "You know, if only I had been able to go to the right schools and meet the right people when I was young, I'd have had chances to improve my cultural abilities. Then I could mingle with people I really want to be with." He had, over the years, completely closed his mind to any present or future development of social graces or the acceptance of ordinary (his term) people and instead threw the blame for his dissatisfaction on the fact that family financial problems had compell d him to attend public schools and state colleges.

A student who failed to graduate expressed regret that she had not attended even two-thirds of the class sessions either because she was unable to get up on time or was simply truant. She said her life was ruined; she would always be a failure. Her inability to accept the fact that the past could not be changed made her refuse to use alternate opportunities which would have enabled her to get her diploma later.

A woman whose marriage seemed doomed said unhappily, "If only I had married Tom instead of Jim! I had my chance six years ago, but I made the wrong choice. Now it's too late for happiness. I know Tom would have been more tender with me, more thoughtful. But he's happily married to someone else now, and I have nothing." She did not stop to think about action she herself could take to strengthen that faltering marriage but instead dwelt only on the past. I could not help feeling somewhat sorry for Jim in this situation.

A man of fifty expressed regret that he had not gone into another line of work instead of business management after he left college. He was now dissatisfied with what he was doing, what he had accomplished, what his chances for the future were. If only he had gone into that other field of endeavor, everything would be perfect today, he was sure. He might be a millionaire, or at least far better off financially than he now was; he knew he would be happier; he probably would have become famous. However, he had consistently failed to use the opportunities his current occupation opened up for him.

The mother of a woman in her early forties passed away after a brief illness. The relationship between the two women had always been strained, even from the time of the woman's adolescence, and disharmony had spoiled their later years. Often they had argued bitterly. After the mother's death, the daughter felt regret that she had never really understood her mother's point of view. Now that she was herself the mother of a teen-ager, she found she had acquired an entirely different perspective on many of the disagreements between herself and her mother. But all the regret she expressed so sorrowfully could not change the past. She blamed herself so excessively that she was no longer able to cope with the daily problems she faced with her own daughter.

The parents of children who had grown up and moved away

found themselves regretting the many times they had been "too busy" to listen to their sons and daughter. They felt the relationship with them now would be much stronger if only they themselves had been more receptive and understanding when the youngsters had wanted to talk things over. Though family communication was restored, they still felt unhappy over the lack of it during their children's more formative years.

An alcoholic or drug addict might regret that he ever took his first drink or "fix," yet be unwilling or even unable to force himself to do anything now to help his problem.

After the great Alaskan earthquake, a woman who lived with her husband in Anchorage feared the possibilities of additional earthquakes and decided to fly back to the "Lower 48" to stay with her parents in Illinois until her husband's job was completed. She was killed in the wreck of the plane carrying her back. Her husband regrets not being more persuasive or forceful in prevailing upon her to stay. "If only I had been more insistent," he says, and as time passes he blames himself more and more.

Examples of regret, vain regret, could go on. Some are mild, almost a nostalgia for things of the past. These *if only's* are harmless, a part of growing older, an indication of the passing of time and our awareness of that passing. As Tennyson writes, "Tears rise in the heart . . . thinking of the days that are no more."

Other regrets may be sharper, yet from them we have learned lessons for both the present and the future. While more painful than nostalgia, such backward looks can be useful and helpful as long as we keep their message in mind.

The regrets that slow us down, inhibit our ability to face life as it truly is today, fill life with sorrow, and endanger relationships with family and friends are the ones we must bring under control.

Regret is a favorite topic of writers, perhaps because of its very universality. Richard Le Gallienne, in his poem "Regret," writes:

> One asked of Regret,
> And I made reply:
> To have held the bird,
> And let it fly.[2]

Novelists use the emotion as a theme to show the devastating results of dwelling on what cannot be changed, results stretching from generation to generation. Psychiatrists record numerous patients' problems which stem from this sore spot in their lives.

Is there a way to help overcome or even eradicate the vain, harmful regrets that plague us? Here are a few suggestions which can offer assistance if considered seriously.

Dealing with Regrets

First must be the *conscious*, admitted realization that what is past is indeed over. To use a cliché, you cannot turn back the clock. Once you accept this fact, you can proceed to the next step. Science fiction stories to the contrary, you are in the present now and, barring catastrophe, will move on into the future. While what you do today may relate to the past, the circumstances, conditioning, and perspective are different. The effort you make to put the past aside will be well worth the price paid in emotional discipline.

Helen knew her parents had planned a college education for her, and, until she met Bob, she had been more than willing to go—in fact, she had already sent in her application. But Bob

2. Richard Le Gallienne, "Regret," in *A Victorian Anthology 1837-1895*, Edmund Clarence Stedman, ed. (Boston: Houghton Mifflin Co., 1895).

swept her off her feet that spring and summer, and they decided not to wait to marry. A few years later she realized that advanced education would give her not only more of a sense of personal fulfillment but also would provide a better way for her to earn a living if anything should happen to Bob or if they should need additional money. Instead of constantly voicing her regret, which certainly would not have helped her marriage, she, at a considerable amount of inconvenience to herself, for she now had a small child, went to college on a part-time basis, eventually earning her degree.

Once you have acknowledged that the past cannot be changed, set your priorities for today. Helen did this, setting up certain goals for herself. Edward Fitzgerald's translation of the *Rubáiyát* of Omar Khayyám requests:

> Ah . . . fill the Cup that clears
> To-DAY of past Regrets and future Fears . . .

Live in the present on a day-to-day basis, guarding against those things which you perceive as incipient regrets. Action should be positive, with the inner realization that today's action cannot be changed tomorrow. If mistakes are made, as they undoubtedly will be, they do not presage the end of the world, of your future, or even of your happiness. Be willing to acknowledge that you too can and will make mistakes, some of which you will simply have to accept as they come.

In attempting to set goals for your future, waste no time in considering what those goals *might* have been "if only . . ." Your potential is great, and you must use your energy to fulfill it instead of bemoaning what has already happened.

Healing Helps

1. Accept the fact that you cannot change what has already occurred.
2. Become active in *today's* projects and plans. Today is, after all, the first day of the rest of your life.
3. Keep your priorities in mind as you carry on the work of the present.
4. Be flexible enough to change your plans and accept alternatives, if necessary, without yielding to the tendency to hold your original ideas as objects for future regret.

STRESS

10 *Conquering that Uptight Feeling*

A letter to Dr. George Thosteson appeared in his daily newspaper column: "I had X rays of my stomach and went through a gastroscopy test with a gastric biopsy. The diagnosis was hypertrophic gastritis. I was told this was caused by my being nervous and upset. I am now 37 years old. The pain in my stomach is almost unbearable at times. I've been on medication for this. Can you tell me something about the condition?"

The doctor answered the patient by defining *gastritis* as an inflamation of the inner wall of the stomach and *hypertrophic* as an enlargement whereby the folds of the stomach lining have become thickened. "The cause," wrote the doctor, "is not known, although it is usually accompanied by excessive secretion of stomach acid and digestive enzymes. The abnormal acidity of the stomach juices could cause your distress. And since gastric secretions are controlled in part by the nervous system, it is possible that your emotional makeup could be at the bottom of your problem."

In addition to medication, he suggested "an attempt to avoid any stressful situations."

No doubt we have all gone through certain times when it seems as if someone has kicked us in the stomach. Such a feeling may occur just before a "stressful" situation or at the time of its occurrence. There are degrees of this disagreeable feeling. Sometimes it can be compared to butterflies flitting about the midsection; at other times it may be less easily described and pinpointed.

I know that when I am to give a lecture or sermon, I invariably ask my wife how I ever allowed myself to be talked into agreeing to appear. It is not that I have no desire to speak before an audience or a congregation but rather the uncomfortable feeling which frequently accompanies the event. Margie usually responds by calmly pointing out that I always say this, have given thousands of talks or sermons, and "You will do all right. You always have." Seasoned actors and performers of other sorts have undergone similar reactions, according to their interviews.

Stress is a familiar word. In engineering parlance, it is caused by tension, compression, or fear, or by a combination of these factors, usually measured in pounds per square inch. The engineering term fittingly describes the intensity with which nontechnical strain acts on us in the pressure of life. Stress can be such an integral part of our daily experiences that we may barely realize we are under stress at all.

Our schedules are so full we do not have time to finish everything on our list. At the end of a busy day, we ask, "What have I really done today?" People honk and glare at us as we rush from work in our car or push for seats in the bus and subway. At home, we find a check we deposited at the bank the previous night has gone astray, the electric dryer appears to have a life of its own and starts up for no reason at all, an attack of gout sidelines the man of the house, and the dog has a bad case of ticks. Such unexpected occurrences make us edgy and interrupt our already hectic flow of life. Frayed tempers

erupt. Boredom simmers into crabbiness. Stress is om-
nipresent. How can we cope?

Symptoms of Stress

Stress, probably more than any other factor, determines the
point at which we find ourselves on the slide down the slope
from health to illness. Stress is not unique to our own country
or time, but, given our way of living, we could fairly accurately label it an "American disease." Let's look at our
nation's background to see why this is so.

One factor is the urge to achieve. At a symposium held in
conjunction with the American Revolution Bicentennial, one
of the questions discussed by a panel attempting to reassess
American values and culture was, "Why do Americans have
such a strong impulse to get ahead?"

One conclusion was that the Quakers and Puritans who
talked about salvation by faith nevertheless behaved as
though temporal works were ultimately the true measure of
heavenly esteem. These early settlers worked hard, were
ambitious and frugal. And many prospered.

The secular types who came to the New World hoped to do
good by doing well. They had the drive to get ahead. If they
did not already have the drive, society motivated them to get
it. Idleness was frequently considered a sin and sometimes
even a crime. Ben Franklin helped establish laziness as a vice in
our national consciousness.

Drive led men like Lewis and Clark to hack their way
through a wilderness; women like Jane Addams to minister
tirelessly to the slum dwellers in Chicago; the Wright brothers
to prove that man can fly, though not like birds; Sabin and
Salk to conquer polio. Individuals such as Henry Ford put the

automobile within the reach of nearly everyone's pocketbook. We thank Clarence Birdseye for many a dinner as he revolutionized the concept of preserving food. Who hasn't been grateful on a hot and humid summer day for Willis H. Carrier after the banner first went up some twenty-five years ago on a Times Square marquee: "Refrigeration cooled."

At one point in recent history, many individuals felt we had entered an era they called the Age of Hesitancy. Some have given up on the rush and push of daily living, but I believe most of us have shoved that feeling aside; it doesn't take long to get back into the intensely competitive world. Somehow, we can't forget it—it blares at us on television and radio, it is plastered on subway billboards, we hear it in the marketplace. "Do you want to get ahead?"

As a result of the push we have had from history, with due consideration for all the benefits it has brought us, stress has become a way of life. Dr. Eugene Jennings, management consultant and advisor to executives, has pointed out that people suffer from energy fatigue and, unable to draw on nonexistant resources, simply plug away with little success.

Some take a drastic step. Eli M. Black had risen from poverty on New York's lower east side to become an orthodox rabbi. He was also an executive with the worry-free comfort of two homes and a chauffeur. He had a family. He had attained an eminent position in the city's business establishment and took part in its philanthropic and intellectual life. He was chairman of a two-billion-dollar conglomerate. Despite all this, Mr. Black, according to the media, committed suicide at the age of fifty-three by leaping through a window of his office in the Pan Am Building.

Dr. Burton L. Nackerson, a psychiatrist, in commenting about suicide said that among the causes of depression "is a sudden feeling of failure because a person hasn't lived up to his aspirations. Defeat leads to a person's perception of himself as being diminished and debased because he was not able to do what he wanted."

We might be tempted to say complacently, "Well, I'm glad I'm not caught up in such a competitive drive to win at all costs." But we are all subject to the ravages of stress. We would like to think that stress is revealed in others only, but such an assumption is false.

We see, hear, and read primarily about the well-publicized executive stress, the urge to get ahead in the business and social world. We forget the stresses afflicting the most ordinary individual.

In addition to that "go, go, go" incentive, the major cause of stress and energy fatigue is years of doing unpleasant jobs, forcing the body forward as if it were some kind of mechanical machine. As a result, the attempt to climb has left the body without reserve fuel. Burned out in the workaday scramble, both executive and worker become unable to achieve, and they can't understand why.

Certain warning signs indicate destructive stress.

1. *Stress symptoms surface in marriage problems and difficulties with children.* Annoying habits, unimportant in themselves, add up to trouble. The husband unloads his pockets on the recently cleaned-off dining room table; family members appear to regard any flat surface as an open invitation to place something on it; the toilet seat is left up in the middle of the night to the consternation of the unwary; dirty dishes remain in the sink; one or more family members habitually are late for everything, including meals. Constant nagging or criticism regarding these habits only compounds the difficulty.

2. *The inability to concentrate for any length of time can be a sign of unusual stress.* This becomes evident in the case of illness or serious financial crisis. Regardless of earnest efforts to keep our minds fixed on the problem at hand, a swarm of

unconnected thoughts takes over. Everything seems hopeless.

3. *Constant and easy loss of temper shows us we are under strain.* Occasional temper blowups can be expected, but when they become frequent, watch out, especially where there is no really justifiable cause for that anger.

4. *Another indication of stress is a vague, unhappy feeling for which there seems to be no real reason.* A friend recently confided to me that he simply hated to face each day because he was unable to feel anything but gloom or foreboding. He could think of nothing that had brought on this feeling, but he simply could not shake it. He wanted to withdraw from society completely, but this wasn't feasible for he had family and business obligations.

5. *Frequent insomnia should be regarded with suspicion.* An occasional bout with this annoying and frustrating situation is of no great concern, to be sure. A certain problem might require resolution the next day; an eagerly anticipated event precludes sleep; an appointment early the next morning must be kept; we have eaten well but not too wisely the night before. We can understand these reasons for either being unable to fall asleep at all or waking in the middle of the night, unable to go back to sleep regardless of how we try.

Chronic sleeplessness, however, is not so easily explained away. We try to stretch out the day, feeling sleep will surely overtake us, but it does not. Morning finds us exhausted, certainly not prepared to face another day of stress and strain. Any of the jumble of ideas which passed through our minds in those wakeful hours fade away.

6. *Moods tend to rise and fall rapidly in a sort of yo-yo fashion when we are under stress.* We go from extreme joy or exhilaration to the depths of despair, again without apparent logical reason.

7. *Stress situations can arouse the "I am always right" syndrome.* While a child may constantly assert that he is

always right and others are wrong, a mature adult should realize that all people make mistakes and a child is no exception. A constantly defensive attitude indicates something is wrong, and tension may very well be that "something wrong."

8. *Look for stress when you have numerous aches and pains for which the doctor or extensive tests find no physical cause.* A physician takes a serious view of the stress his patient is under and may advise certain relaxants or refer the patient to a specialist in psychosomatic illnesses.

Ways to Deal with Stress

As we have seen, stress can be helpful if we know how to use it. It becomes a friend when we learn to cope with it.

One of the first things to realize is that we will not go through life on an even keel. We must expect some ups and downs. There are too many stresses and strains in our body's physical, mental, and chemical reactions for us to expect our boat not to rock. Handling the stresses as they come along so that we benefit from them will help level off those crests and troughs and give us the opportunity to achieve goals instead of merely floundering along.

A psychiatrist has pointed out that the average individual is likely to have three to five real stress situations in his lifetime. These, of course, vary from individual to individual, but we will consider a few more common ones. The stress of school, whether the student is at the top, middle, or bottom of the class, provides an early one. Today's students have many more stresses placed upon them than did previous generations of school-goers. And the students' stresses frequently become those of parents and teachers as well.

Another serious stress situation might be in the area of romance. An unhappy love affair or a broken marriage certainly places strains on those involved. Simply adjusting to marriage itself might be classified in the same way. Job security, or rather the lack of it, may compound numerous other problems. And, of course, the loss of a loved one, whether by death or separation, is frequently a crisis situation.

Another fact we must face is that no simple solutions or easy ways to rid oneself of stress are likely to present themselves. As a matter of fact, we no doubt would be in worse condition if we had no stress at all. But there are a few things we can do to help heal this particular sore spot when it gets to be too much for us and threatens to take us over, when it disrupts our living and our relationships with others.

The majority of our stresses are minor ones, and if we try to develop a feeling of confidence in our own ability to deal with them, success is more certain. The problem exists, to be sure, and something must be done about it, but we need not feel helpless.

Keeping things in the proper perspective helps. Without perspective we lose direction, questioning our own resources and allowing stress to take us over so that we function poorly or not at all. In such a case we may retreat inward and sever ourselves from valuable links with reality.

A successful elderly businessman said, "I have more get-up-and-go now than when I was forty-five. It's because I've continued to hold to that mental attitude quoted in the story about the little train, which I read frequently to my grandchildren: "I think I can; I think I can."

Coping positively with stress requires both hope and optimism.

One of the questions often put forth in doctors' forums is that of fatigue or loss of energy. People want help to overcome that dragged-out, weary, headachy feeling which takes enjoyment out of their lives. How does the body produce energy? How can one increase his feeling of well-being? Why should a person feel tired when there is no apparent cause?

What can a person do beyond the annual medical checkup, a balanced diet, rest, and exercise?

Stress can cause a mental fatigue that is hard to separate from physical weariness, "All work and no play makes Jack [or Jill] a dull boy [or girl, as the case may be]" applies here. Do you take vacations, even short ones, away from your regular routine? Do you take time to mix socially with friends? Or are you constantly bored, whether at work or in other situations? Boredom itself is a potent cause of stress and fatigue. A person doing effortless but unchallenging work can appear as exhausted at the end of the day as someone doing heavy but interesting things. As a matter of fact, the person doing the heavy work can recover from his fatigue over a shorter period of time.

Boredom, rather than long hours of heavy responsibility is a major source of stress for American workers. In a survey of 2,010 individuals in jobs ranging from factory hands to family physicians, the researchers found that the workers trapped in dull, repetitive jobs suffered far more occupational stress, even though they put in fewer work hours. It was found, too, that job stress causes anxiety, depression, and irritation.

The same study revealed that job satisfaction was tied to the opportunity of the worker to use his skills or participate in decision-making. Family physicians, working an average of fifty-five hours a week, reported the least emotional strain and fewer physical problems. Assembly line workers encountered the greatest strain with job dissatisfaction as well as physical and emotional complaints. Job insecurity and lack of social support from co-workers appeared to be the main causes of occupational stress.

Not everyone can have a creative job bringing new situations each day. The next best thing is to get away for awhile, perhaps for a long weekend away from one's usual setting. Even a few hours can be of help. Personally, I get relaxation merely looking around for an hour or two in a large do-it-yourself department store. Buying a few inexpensive items makes my visit even more invigorating. We must learn to recharge our energy batteries by getting away, losing ourselves in something different, relaxing, forgetting the cares of our workaday world. Refreshed, we can then return to responsibilities with vigorous enthusiasm.

The ability to loaf constructively is not as easy as it sounds. Too much inactivity can create a stress situation in itself. However, if a person finds he is unable to sit down for a short time or stop for a cup of coffee without feeling uncomfortable, he is making a mistake. A few minutes each day doing absolutely nothing could be the very medicine he needs to help him approach the difficult problem with new insight and vigor. The practice of quiet meditation has become increasingly popular and helpful in recent years.

The Japanese paraphrase of the 23rd Psalm by Toki Miyashina puts it this way:

> The Lord is my pacesetter, I shall not rush;
> He makes me stop and rest for quiet intervals.
> He provides me with images of stillness,
> which restore my serenity;
> He leads me in ways of efficiency
> through calmness of mind,
> And this guidance is peace.
> Even though I have a great many things
> to accomplish this day,
> I will not fret, for his presence is here.
> His timelessness, his all-importance,
> will keep me in balance.
> He prepares refreshment and renewal
> in the midst of my activity
> By anointing my mind with his oils of tranquility.
> My cup of joyous energy overflows.

Surely harmony and effectiveness
shall be the fruits of my hours,
For I shall walk in the pace of my Lord,
and dwell in his heaven forever.[1]

Life, with all its problems, should be a pleasant experience, lived out in health and optimism. Give yourself a chance to learn the art of occasional loafing.

It helps you to have one close friend with whom to share the details of your life. In youth, it is not too difficult to have a network of friends with whom to discuss your stress situations, common to many of your peers. But as you become older, you need the more solid support of one or a few confidants with whom you can be yourself. Sharing crises or stresses can help cushion them.

The person or persons in whom you confide might be a doctor, your mate, a psychiatrist, a social worker, a guidance counselor, a member of the clergy, a close friend. Such an individual will want to help you and will listen with sympathy and understanding. If the person in whom you confide cannot help you himself, he may be able to refer you to someone who can. Conversely, you can help your friends by being the kind of confidant they need in their times of stress.

Dr. Elisabeth Kübler-Ross is the Swiss psychiatrist who has ministered to hundreds of dying patients. When she first came to America, the only place she could find employment was in the schizophrenic ward of a New York hospital where she soon discovered that what she had learned in books was of little help to her. Not knowing what else to do, she listened to the patients. The result was that 94 percent of the cases, considered hopeless at one time, were eventually discharged.

1. *Psalm 23* by Toki Miyashina. Copyright by K. H. Strange. (Edinburgh: The Saint Andrew Press, 1963).

Sports help a person to avoid feeling strained and pressured. Exercise, when not carried to the extreme, may be of help. There are so many types of sports in vogue now that it should not be difficult to find one suitable to your taste and ability.

Flexibility is a must in avoiding stress situations. In these days, jobs are established or wiped out quickly in corporate headquarters. Those who cannot adapt fold under the stress both physically and emotionally.

For fifty years my father, who began work at fourteen, was employed in the pipe-making division of U.S. Steel. At first he worked in the lap mills, but when that type of pipe was phased out, he was transferred to the butt weld mill, having to learn a new process. But along came technology with automation, computors, programmers, new machines, and new methods. Whereas it had once taken thirty men to work a pipe-making furnace, the work now could be done by three or four men. My father was passed over and younger men trained in the operation of the new mill were hired. My father was discouraged. Although he was transferred to the seamless mill, he finally sought early retirement. Emotionally he was done in, for he could not adjust.

It pays to stay loose and improve skills with the hope that a dead-end job is indeed not the end. It can be a stepping-stone to something better. With this outlook, the stress situation is eased.

What are your priorities? Do you stick with them or do you vacillate? A speaker once described life as a chair. The "chair of life" has four legs—vocation, avocation, rest and recreation, and religion. If one leg, such as work, becomes longer than the others, it throws the whole chair off balance. Anyone who has tried to remedy such a situation with a real chair knows what can happen. You can easily wind up with a stool instead of a chair.

Bringing work home from the office night after night, attending organizational meetings in so-called free time, and becoming too completely involved in community life can lead to unusual stress. It is far better to set your priorities and live a full, joyful, and enriching life.

Healing Helps

Go to your local public library and pick up a book which teaches systems of relaxation. One such publication is *Escape from Stress* by Kenneth Lamott (Putnam). He suggests various methods of yoga, hypnosis, transcendental meditation, and other disciplines. Relaxation systems are as precise as ballet or tennis.

A few simple exercises are as follows:

1. Sit on the edge of a chair with feet apart, slanting forward. Sit straight. Close your eyes. Now collapse in the manner of a rag doll with head forward, spine rounded, hands on knees. Repeat, "My right arm is heavy," mentally for twenty seconds. Drop your arm to your side. Concentrate on your arm from armpit to fingers. Make a fist, flex your arms, take a deep breath, and open your eyes. Repeat the procedure with your left arm, doing the entire exercise three or four times a day. Gradually try the same procedure in relaxing each leg.

2. Twice a day, lie on your back on the floor with your head slightly raised on a pillow. Your spine should be straight. The knees are bent and the feet are placed about eight inches apart. Put one hand on the stomach; the chest should not move. After several tries, smile slightly, breath in through the nose and out through the mouth. Whisper a sound such as "haaaaaaah," which will sound like the wind. Mouth, jaw, tongue are loose and without strain. Take long, slow breaths

into the stomach. Do this for five or ten minutes at a time. Follow with about ten breaths deep into your lungs. When you become proficient (for it takes a bit of practice), you can practice the exercise whenever you feel tenseness creeping over you.

3. For further relaxation exercises, see *Learning How to Relax*, Volume XXV, Number 1, published by Blue Cross, 840 N. Lake Shore Drive, Chicago, Illinois 60611.

INGRATITUDE

11   *An Attitude of Gratitude*

In a "Peanuts" comic strip, which appears in the *Newark Star Ledger*, by Charles Schulz, Charlie Brown's sister is lamenting, "My life is a drag . . . I'm completely fed up . . . I've never felt so low."

Charlie replies, "When you're in a mood like this, you should try to think of things you have to be thankful for . . . in other words, count your blessings."

"Ha!" retorts Lucy. "That's a good one! I could count my blessings on one finger! I've never had anything, and I never will have anything. I don't get half the breaks that other people do . . . . nothing ever goes right for me! And you talk about counting blessings! You talk about being thankful! What do I have to be thankful for?"

Charlie answers, "Well, for one thing, you have a little brother that loves you . . ."

She looks at him, humbled, then hugs him and begins, as only Lucy can, to cry.[1]

---

1. Text from *Peanuts* by Charles M. Schulz; © 1956, 1963 United Feature Syndicate, Inc.

INGRATITUDE

One reason so many of us appreciate "Peanuts" is the perception Charles Schulz shows. He continues to stab our consciences, touching our feelings, actions, and problems in his own gentle way. We see ourselves in Lucy.

We do indeed find ourselves in troubled times. A rapid rise in unemployment, threatening war clouds, the toll of inflation, the constant barrage of bad news often overwhelms us to the point where we feel there is nothing to be thankful for. In addition, our personal lives give us cause for discouragement. We can think of others far less deserving (in our estimation) who are more fortunate than we. Then someone reminds us, in the broadest sense, that, "You have a little brother that loves you!"

Disaster may disintegrate our faith. A member of one of my congregations was suddenly stricken with a terminal illness of the fast-growing type. In a few weeks, her husband was a widower with three small children to care for. Our small community was shaken by the swift course of events and the tragedy within that household. Shortly after the services, Fred indicated the bitterness and resentment he felt over what had happened; he did not hesitate to condemn a God who, he felt, had done this to him capriciously, without reason. "I don't want your God," he said over and over again. He harbored that resentment for as long as I knew him; everything about his life was embittered. He was struggling in a hostile world where he had nothing to be thankful for.

Such need not be the case. At about the same time, in that particular congregation, a ten-year-old girl contracted polio and for weeks hovered between life and death. Her mother spent all her waking moments beside her child's hospital bed; her father was there every afternoon after work and throughout the evening. We all prayed for Linda's recovery, for the community was a close-knit one. But the child's life ebbed, and she died. Bitterness? No, though it was with sorrow that Elsie and Don said good-bye to their only daughter. They did not forget God in their extreme anguish, nor did they turn against him. Their attitude was that they had had Linda for ten years; they still had a young son; they had each other; they had the love of God and their many friends. How often are we truly grateful for what we do have, or do we forget our blessings when misfortune strikes?

In a novel that caught the public's emotions a few years ago, Erich Segal presented a fast-moving account of the love and marriage of Oliver and Jenny in *Love Story*. In the novel, the twenty-four-year-old Jenny is dying of leukemia. Oliver says, "I began to think about God. . . . Not because I wanted to strike him in the face, to punch him out for what he was about to do, . . . I hoped there was a God I could say 'thank you' to. 'Thank you for letting me wake up and see Jennifer.' "[2]

A lonely, gentle, talented man who had to cope with caring for a beloved sister in her ever-increasing bouts of insanity, Charles Lamb once wrote, "I own that I am disposed to say grace upon twenty other occasions in the course of the day besides my dinner. I want a form for setting out upon a pleasant walk, for a moonlight ramble, for a friendly meeting, or a solved problem. Why have we none for books, those spiritual repasts—a grace before Milton—a grace before Shakespeare?"

I first read those words of Lamb's many years ago, and I have since thought about them in the most unusual places. In the summer of 1974 my wife and I traveled to Alaska. One of the wonders of the world I had especially wanted to see was Mt. McKinley. As we flew from Anchorage to Nome, high above the cloud cover, the pilot announced that we could see the top of McKinley rising majestically above the clouds. It was a glorious sight, but I was not satisfied. I wanted to take pictures of this marvel of nature from the ground.

On the day we were scheduled to travel close to the

2. Erich Segal, *Love Story* (New York: New American Library, 1970).

mountain, broken clouds appeared early in the morning. The bus ride was anything but comfortable, the weather turned cold and windy, but I did not care. Ahead was that big, beautiful mountain, and I would get a breathtaking picture of it. Alas, this was not to be. After those hours of travel, of waiting with camera poised, clouds obscured the view. Like Moses on Mt. Nebo, I felt cheated. I had not seen my "promised land."

Back in the lodge, I suddenly recalled Lamb's words and felt chastened. How easy to resent the lack of fulfillment of my desire, how easy to take my blessings for granted. I remembered all the treasured moments we had had with newfound friends, how many exhilarating views we had been privileged to see, how many fascinating experiences had been ours. Charles Lamb was right; there should be a special grace for every one of those times.

The Alaskan experience was limited in scope. During my entire life, many people have shown their kindness to my family and me, yet I have taken everything for granted! How about the challenging tasks and the help in reaching my goals? Each day brings with it an opportunity to express gratitude, even when the going seems rough.

Gratitude is not a surface emotion. I overheard a father and son talking about their fishing trip as they stood by the shore of a New Hampshire lake. The father, a man of few words, was accustomed to presenting his children with an idea that at the moment seemed beyond their grasp. He would not elaborate but instead let the thought fall into the minds of the youngsters, either to be forgotten or to grow into new concepts as the child matured. On this particular evening, the sky was ablaze with crimson, shading into deep purple. The lake reflected the glory in its still waters. The boy looked out over the scene with awe and said, "Look at that, Dad. Makes you thankful to be alive, doesn't it?"

The father, standing by the boat with an anchor in his hands, silhouetted against all this splendor, smiled as he looked down at his son. "My boy, anyone can be grateful for a sunset."

At the time, I considered this a cynical remark, but upon later reflection, found a more profound idea behind the surface meaning. Anyone can be grateful for the obvious. The father wanted his son to look more deeply, to be grateful for little things as well.

Express Gratitude

The chorus of an old, now seldom sung, gospel hymn tells us:

Count your blessings, name them one by one;
Count your blessings, see what God hath done.[3]

Counting the blessings is not enough; we need to express our gratitude. This gratitude can range from a simple "thank you" to a deep prayer of thankfulness for the privilege of living. Expression of our gratitude to God brings with it various benefits, one of the first being a closer kinship with and understanding of God.

However, God is not the only one to whom we show appreciation. The unexpected "thank you" is most welcome and can give another person an upsurge of feeling, a warm glow that is, in turn, transmitted to still other persons in a sort of chain reaction.

Teachers many times get the feeling that perhaps all their efforts with students have really not been of much avail. They

3. *Tabernacle Hymns Number Three* © Tabernacle Publishing Company, Chicago, Illinois, 1941. Words by Reverend Johnson Oatman, Jr., music by E. O. Excell.

wonder if anything that they have said or done has reached the lives of these young people at all. When my wife received a note from one of her former students, she was moved to tears of happiness. To this day, she treasures that note and others similar to it. The note reads, in part, "I have witnessed and felt your deep and sincere concern for others. This has brought me comfort, happiness, and hope. . . . you have helped me in so many ways. . . . I knew that if I ever turned to you, you would really care. . . .you restored my optimism in mankind. P.S. I hope you are too set in your ways to change."

I once had the occasion to praise a jeweler for some work he had done for me on an antique watch. He beamed and said, "You know, you are the first person to come in here to tell me your watch is running fine. People only come in to growl about how their watches are gaining or losing time. I get all the bad news, but little good. Thank you."

Many letters to the editor come to the magazine for which I work. When an error has been made or a controversial subject introduced, adverse criticism is plentiful. What a welcome relief it is to see letters expressing gratitude for inspiration, a helpful story, a thought-provoking article.

An executive in charge of relief supplies told me that he could recall only a few letters which had come to him expressing gratitude for help given in time of need. There were many complaining about the method of distribution, the quality of material, the time involved in waiting.

Failure to express gratitude is an age-old problem. It has been variously blamed on lack of training as a child, a selfish nature, the rush of the business world, or the pressure of activities. All these reasons may play their respective parts in today's seeming ingratitude, but the basic difficulty lies with man himself, his thoughtlessness, his lack of concern. Jesus, returning to Jerusalem, passed through a certain village. Here ten lepers who had heard of his healing powers came to see him, staying at the proper distance for those afflicted with the dread disease. They called for help, and the Lord, having compassion, healed them. Only one of the ten turned and with a loud voice glorified God and offered thanks. Christ asked, "Were not ten cleansed? Where are the nine?"

Gratitude is expressed in many ways. Our cat rubs his body against my legs and purrs. Our dog wags his tail. Man's own gratitude may be expressed in a letter, by a word or look, with flowers or other gifts, whether inexpensive or costly. The assumption that the expression of gratitude must equal the benefits received is false. The thought, the attempt, the expression, the giving of a part of one's self means most. The expression "The gift without the giver is bare" is true and applies to expressions of appreciation.

An ungrateful person, both in literature and in real life, is regarded with scorn. Shakespeare says:

> Blow, blow, thou winter wind!
> Thou art not so unkind
> As man's ingratitude.
>
> *As You Like It* (Act II, Scene 7)

or

> How sharper than a serpent's tooth it is
> To have a thankless child!
>
> *King Lear* (Act I, Scene 4)

The bard waxes vehement when he says:

> I hate ingratitudes more in a man
> Than lying, vainness, babbling drunkeness,
> Or any taint of vice whose strong corruption
> Inhabits our frail blood.
>
> *Twelfth Night* (Act III, Scene 4)

121

A sensitive awareness of the kindnesses, of the help in time of trouble, of understanding, of gifts both material and spiritual—this response leads to an attitude of gratitude, a delicate flower which needs constant cultivation.

The Joy and Exhilaration of Gratitude

Edwin Arlington Robinson in "Captain Craig" classifies two kinds of gratitude in this way:

> . . . the sudden kind
> We feel for what we take, the larger kind
> We feel for what we give.

The satisfaction a doctor receives when he has brought a patient through a long and difficult illness is one of gratitude as is the feeling a lawyer has when he has successfully defended his client against an unjust accusation. Few of us can be heart specialists like Dr. Michael E. DeBakey or Dr. Christiaan Barnard, but when we make some service to others a natural part of our living, we express gratitude for what we have received. A child's gift to his mother of a picture he himself has drawn pleases not only the mother but the young artist as well. The gift of a theater ticket to a friend who has unfailingly helped out in a family illness speaks volumes and brings a glow to the donor. A thank-you letter or card is inexpensive, but the joy it generates uplifts the spirit.

The Rewards of Gratitude

The happiness of a person shows through his gratitude toward life, other people, and God. Conversely, the gratitude expressed brings happiness to the individual almost as a by-product. In addition, he is most likely to notice other side benefits.

1. *Gratitude cures despair.* We may feel dissatisfied with our lives, believing we have been given a raw deal. We may foresee only a bleak future. Cultivating a grateful attitude brings appreciation of the good things which have come our way, however small they may be. Even the late irascible W.C. Fields once said he never crawled into bed at night without giving thanks for his mattress and clean sheets. As a boy, he had been a part of a poor family where such things were luxuries. Even when he acquired wealth, he did not take them for granted. Gratitude may not bring us material blessings, but it certainly does wonders for our outlook.

2. *Gratitude emphasizes the present.* The lure of nostalgia is a part of the seventies. Looking back with longing has its place, but we live in the present. Gratitude keeps us from falling into remorse over the job we did not get, the girl we lost to someone else, the boy who ran off with another girl, the opportunities we muffed, the blows of unkind words, the bad investment, and the career we started too late.

But the very things we look back on, whether with nostalgia or regret, are the bases of our present. Our gratitude is for what is going on now as well as for what has been done for us and to us in the past. We express gratitude *today*; we live in the present.

3. *Gratitude changes our perspective.* Gratitude may at times be difficult to express, indeed, even to feel. When our little worlds appear to fall apart, gratitude does not come easily. However, showing gratitude for *something* to *someone*, no matter how hard we may have to search for a reason, takes our attention off ourselves. Losing ourselves in concern for another person, letting him know we are grateful for what he has done, helps us see our own difficulties from a different angle. After all, the world does not owe us anything; we have nothing which we did not first receive from others.

INGRATITUDE

Healing Helps

1. Take the time each day to reflect on at least three things for which you are thankful.
2. Express appreciation in some way for each of these things.
3. Send cards or notes of appreciation to persons who are not expecting them.
4. Perform an act of kindness for someone else to brighten his day.
5. Thank God for the many blessings you enjoy each day.

PANIC

12 *Overcoming a Dubious Legacy*

The small town of Amity was nearly paralyzed after the first visit of a shark to its beaches had taken the life of a swimmer. "Sharks in a sea-side resort are like ax murders. People react to them with their guts. There's something crazy and evil and uncontrollable about them. If we tell people there's a killer shark around here, we can kiss the summer good-by." So spoke Harry Meadows in Peter Benchley's superthriller, *Jaws*. The novel takes a panic-producing disaster and shows how a representative cross-section of humanity responds to it.[1]

Panic is that sudden, unreasoning, hysterical fear that spreads quickly. Unfortunately, it is a sore spot, not only on a collective level, but also on an individual level.

The origin of the word *panic* goes back to Greek mythology. Pan, the son of Hermes, was the god of forests and fields, shepherds and flocks. Not only an excellent musician, especially on the shepherd's pipe, he was also gifted in the art of prophecy. As he frequented the mountains of Arcadia in

1. Peter Benchley, *Jaws* (New York: Doubleday and Co., 1974)

Greece, where he tended his herds and flocks, he roamed through the countryside frightening passersby. His presence was thought to inspire such fear that the word *panic* is derived from his name.

Artists have depicted this mischievous being as having a curly beard and the horns, ears, legs, and tail of a goat. Traditionally, the god's death was announced by a mysterious voice heard by a sailor at sea during the reign of Emperor Tiberius in the first century.

While we may not worship Pan and simply regard him as a part of Greek mythology, his legacy of fear lives on in *panic*, which has gradually come to express extreme degrees of fear, alarm, perplexity, dread, and horror.

As far as group panic is concerned, we have seen examples of it on our TV sets, especially at the close of the Vietnam war. The inhabitants of South Vietnam, not knowing, or fearing, what might be in store for them as the army of the North overran the area, frantically sought to escape as the United States was pulling out its personnel. Panic ensued. Thousands of people, clawing, pushing, and shoving, crowded into small boats, ships, airplanes, and helicopters. The news media showed them hanging onto wheels and landing gear of the helicopters as they sought to escape from their homeland, regardless of what might happen to them on foreign soil.

Older people may relate panic to serious depressions in the history of our country, with financial crises preceding these depressions. In the stock market crash of 1929, when nearly 15 million workers no longer had jobs, panic engulfed much of the country.

Group panic tends to spread rapidly. Some years ago there was a tragic fire in the Coconut Grove nightclub in Boston. Most of the people who died then died needlessly. They panicked, and all rushed at once for the exits. As a result, the passageways were blocked and people were literally trampled to death.

Natural disasters have resulted in group panic. The words fire, flood, earthquake, hurricane, and tornado inspire terror in the collective and individual mind.

A panic-stricken individual knows extreme fear, regardless of whether he is in a group or not. I personally can recall some minutes of panic on a PATH train from Hoboken, New Jersey, to Penn Station in New York. Since replaced by sleek new cars, the coaches at that time were in terrible condition. I had been on the train when it had to stop for one reason or another before this, but on the day in question, the train ground to a halt while we were under the Hudson River. As usual, the cars were jammed with commuters. The day was hot and humid. At first, the reaction was to loosen ties and remove jackets. Time dragged on. The stale air began to take its toll. I, for one, began to feel panic. I had visions of all of us being asphyxiated before we could get out of the tunnel. I had nearly reached what I thought would be my breaking point when the train started up again.

Panic Reflex

Panic results in a number of reflexes, the most common of which are for flight, frozen immobility, or complete hysteria. Unlike most animals, which have sharp teeth, claws, and speed, we do not have the defense mechanisms to cope with sudden and startling situations, and unless we can mentally control our impulses, more damage results than is otherwise necessary.

The flight reflex can be an ill-considered one. Some reading this chapter may recall 1938 and the announcement by Orson Welles. Over the radio came the news that the United States was being attacked by Martians. The program was only a radio play, but it was so realistically done that those tuning in a little late did not realize the fact. The country was thrown into a state of panic. People leaped into their cars, not even sure where they were headed. Some attempted suicide. Others fled to attics and basements. When the same program was repeated in Quito, Ecuador, people panicked there as well, and later were so enraged that they destroyed the local radio station and newspaper.

The radio play was imaginary, but real terrorizing situations have resulted in bizarre reactions as well. In the case of earthquakes, some people have leaped blindly into the fissures. On the occasion of fire, others have rushed back into the inferno after being led to safety.

Inadvertently, newspapers, radio, and television have themselves created panic at times. Bad news is attention-getting and good news is not. Sometimes the bad news becomes exaggerated and out of focus because of rumors or overemphasis, and some people begin to get that feeling of panic.

Panic can lead to suicide. After the first huge bombardments of Cologne during World War II, many individuals drowned themselves in the river. The same reaction has occurred on ships that have caught fire at sea. While there has been the possibility that all passengers could be saved, some have preferred to surrender immediately to death in the sea. People have leaped to certain death from burning buildings when help was available—if they had only waited a few more minutes.

Reports have been given of people who froze into immobility when they saw a car approaching them; instead of trying to leap out of the way, they have remained transfixed in one place, unable to save themselves.

Hysteria is the reaction of some to a projected danger. Central and northern Ohio is sometimes called Tornado Alley. As I headed north from Cincinnati in 1975, I noted the sky getting darker and darker toward the west. On the radio, tornado warnings came every few seconds. "Tornado alert!"

Like many other drivers, I pulled alongside the highway and waited uneasily until the storm funnel had passed. In the meantime, some of the people had become hysterical.

Fear for the future can lead to panic. In one of my early pastorates, a church member attempted to end his life by shooting himself. He was unsuccessful in this and was taken to the hospital, where he responded to treatment. When he was well enough to talk, he spoke freely to me about his motive. He had had a losing year in his little grocery business, as large supermarkets began springing up in the area. He panicked. No longer could he cope with the fear and expectation that he would be driven out of business. He preferred to take his own life.

Interestingly enough, a number of bodily changes occur as a result of panic. An unexpected or unknown threat can result in diarrhea. People may prattle foolishly or giggle like children, unable to control themselves in the face of disaster. Psychiatrists claim that in moments of extreme danger and fear the sexual urge increases. During wartime, they say, it is a common experience behind the battlefront, as if the instinct for reproduction speaks more loudly with the imminent possibility of death.

Several years ago a widespread blackout of the eastern portion of the United States occurred. People were trapped in elevators, subways, and skyscrapers. Nine months later, the newspapers reported a tremendous jump in the birth rate. It may have been an unscientific conclusion, but the sudden rise in the number of births was attributed to the panic engendered by the blackout.

How to Cope with Panicky Situations

1. *To cope with panic, prepare for eventualities.* In the building where I work we have a fire drill once a month. All of us on the eighteenth floor know exactly what our plan of exit is

to be in case of an emergency. Some of my colleagues take this matter nonchalantly and others refuse to participate in drills at all. Frankly, I take the drills seriously because I know they will help me, as well as others, avoid panic if sudden evacuation of the building should become necessary.

At the beginning of a pleasure cruise, one of the first directives the passengers receive is instructions on how to don their life jackets and where to gather by the lifeboats. Schools have, by law, required numbers of monthly fire drills. In Bloomfield, New Jersey, for example, some fifteen hundred students can leave the building in an orderly fashion in a matter of minutes. When air raids were considered imminent, drills were held so that students would know just where to go for maximum safety.

By preparing mentally for extreme eventualities, we are better able to deal with them when and if they do come upon us.

2. *Keep informed and insist on being kept abreast of what is happening.* Fortunately, communication today lets us know what is going on about us, whether natural phenomena or man-made dangers. "Forewarned is forearmed" applies here. applies here.

3. *Respond to leadership instead of becoming a part of the problem.* Several years ago an incident illustrating this point took place in a theater in one of our midwestern towns. Someone saw a puff of smoke. Frightened, he grabbed the arm of a police officer who happened to be standing nearby and shouted, "Fire!" The officer responded by leaping on the seat, removing his pistol from its holster and calling out to the people who were already yielding to panic, "Everyone stand in his place!" His appearance was so threatening, so fascinating, and so commanding that, though the flames could already be seen at the side of the stage, everyone obeyed the orders of the young officer. He gave concise instructions to evacuate the most dangerous places first, but his hand, brandishing the

pistol, served as a warning to any others tempted to push their way out before told to do so. The orderly evacuation continued despite the sound of flames and the collapse of wooden structures behind the stage. No shouting or crying was heard. By the time the flames had reached the wooden ceiling, all the people were gone.

Cabin attendants in airplanes are trained to exude confidence and capability in the face of possible danger. Frequent newspaper accounts attest to the efficacy of this training.

4. *Don't give up hope.* When an oil drilling rig toppled in the Gulf of Mexico, five men were trapped inside. Things looked almost hopeless for their survival. But when divers went down to rescue the supposedly lost men, all were found alive. One of them in an interview said it was a miracle that they were saved. "But," he said, "I believe in miracles."

We can adjust to serious, adverse circumstances if we keep our cool. We can bear up under hunger, famine, sorrow, disease, and poverty. We can endure an untold amount of suffering. All this we can do if we keep hope alive.

Healing Helps

1. Insofar as possible, make advance preparations for dealing with possible catastrophes.
2. Make a conscious effort to remain calm if disaster does strike.
3. Believe in miracles.
4. Do not give up hope.
5. Keep your faith that God is close to you.

GRIEF

 *Walk Through the Dark Shade*

"If the internal griefs of every man could be read, written on his forehead, how many who now excite envy would appear to be objects of pity!" This quotation from "Without and Within" by Pierre Metastasio[1] clearly illustrates the privacy of grief, but it also intimates the universality of this particular sore spot. Grief differs from sorrow only in its intensity and brings with it great emotional suffering. Like many of our other problems, this particular one comes to everyone at some time or another, and, being individuals, we react to it in varying ways. No person can tell another precisely how to deal with grief. As Shakespeare put it: "Everyone can master a grief but he that has it." One thing we have in common, however, is that we are never quite prepared, even though we realize its inevitability.

A frequent cause for grief is the death of a loved one, though this is by no means the only cause. When the South Vietnam

1. Pierre Metastastio, "Without and Within," Paul Carroll, ed. (Chicago: Follett Publishing Co., 1968).

embassy closed its doors, Miss Nguyen Thi Phuong Dung, the second secretary and political officer, said in a newspaper account, "It was like half of your life dying. . . . When I was young, I didn't know what dying was like. I know now. You emerge from the grave and see everything differently. You see people differently." Severe material losses, such as losing a job or losing everything in a disaster, bring despair, frustration, and anguish. But regardless of the bleak outlook, there is always the possibility that the future could remedy the situation. Grief as a result of a death has a particularly traumatic impact. Death seems so final; the one we love is gone and we remain. How shall we cope with our grief? The one we care for is afflicted painfully, irremediably; how can we endure seeing that person suffer?

When grief comes into our own lives, our first reaction is complete disbelief, if only for a short time. Heartbreak comes to someone else, not to *us*. Somehow our situation is unique; no one truly understands our emotions; no one can help; there is absolutely nothing ahead for us.

In this chapter we will consider the reactions to grief, steps in adjustment to it, and even the positive aspects of such intense sorrow. We hope that, through a careful examination of these areas, we will be able to come to grips with our own personal griefs and see them, not as destructive forces that conquer us, but rather as challenges and stepping-stones to more meaningful lives. We do not seek to forget our deep sorrow completely, for this is impossible. Rather we seek to accept it and use the experience positively.

Reactions

Studies and experience have shown there are certain generalized reactions to grief, whatever its cause. These reactions vary in the length of time they endure and in intensity, because, as we have noted, individuals differ in personality and background. Some individuals, unfortunately, carry certain reactions with them, and the remainder of their lives is spent in mourning and regret. A whole chapter could be written simply on the psychological reasons why this is so. Suffice it to say that the reactions themselves are normal and natural—nature's way of helping us heal a severe emotional wound.

Already mentioned is the first reaction of shock, the inability to comprehend what has happened. This is not real; it cannot be happening to *me*. I have read about such things, and I have pitied those to whom it happened, but somehow it shouldn't happen to *me*—I am different. Unreality and numbness surround me.

My wife and I felt this way when our young son died suddenly following a brief illness. Certainly I, as a pastor, had been in homes where children had died. Only a few years before, close friends had lost a daughter to polio, and we had grieved with them. I knew the accepted responses—God's will, meeting again in heaven, no longer having to face the troubles of the world, the blessing of having other children left to us—I knew all this. But he was *our* son, not someone else's son—*our* son had died. At first we could not accept, *would* not accept that fact. And may I interject here the comment that until one has been in a similar situation, he does not know with certainty just how he will respond. He may know how he would *like* to respond, how he *should* respond, but not how he *will* respond.

Friends of ours have suffered grief over their teen-age son who left home and turned to hard drugs. For months on end, they do not know where he is. There is an occasional postcard, but he moves on. Their grief is a continuing thing, but their first response was utter disbelief. *Their* son would never do anything like this—but he did.

The same feeling of shock came to a young couple who lived near us in a small midwestern town years ago. Their son was born a mongoloid, and at that time it was felt nothing could be done for such children except to institutionalize them. After nine months of hoping, planning, rejoicing in the fact that after five years of marriage they would at last have a child, this had happened.

So it goes—we are not prepared, we cannot accept what is fact. And there are many, many more areas in which grief finds us vulnerable.

After the initial period of shock comes a time when we are unable to concentrate on anything else. We may return to work, we may resume household duties, we may converse on various surface topics, but our whole inner being is torn with what has happened in our lives. Inexplicably, we find our-selves resenting even the most well-meant condolences or attempts to help. Nothing else is of importance any longer. We read the same lines in books and letters without com-prehension. Television, movies, the theater hold no interest. At the very center of our being is a desolate awareness of a permanent end to a relationship.

Sometimes, as sensibility to the world around us returns, we feel hostile—toward God, who allowed this to occur; surely he should have done *something*; toward the doctor, who ought to have been able to find a cure or who could have operated sooner; toward other persons, who dare to go on about their business as if the world had not suddenly crashed down over us. We are bitter at the lot fate has cast for us; we do not understand *why*. The misfortunes of others pale beside our own. We probably do not verbalize these feelings, except perhaps to an intimate friend, though even that is unlikely. We maintain conventional composure, but bitterness seethes.

On the other hand, instead of hostility, guilt may overtake us. What did we do to anger God? What wrong have we committed that we and our loved one should be so punished? We frantically probe our pasts for the reason.

Parents who have lost children tend to berate themselves for punishing the child at an earlier time. In case of an accident, the "what if" approach is used. What if I had not sent him on that errand—what if I had not insisted she come home this weekend—what if they had caught an earlier plane—what if . . . ? The list is endless, and the pain is endless too if we continue to dwell on it.

The same pattern holds true in the case of terminal illness. If only we had discovered the growth earlier—if only she had gone to the doctor when she first felt ill—if only the new drug had been discovered in time—if only. . .

On occasion, persons faced by inconsolable grief will withdraw entirely from their usual patterns of living, hopeful for only a short period. Somehow life has changed and to go about activities in the customary manner and order appears disloyal. Still others find consolation in the very regularity of a certain pattern of living and refuse to deviate from it.

All of these reactions—shock, lack of concentration, guilt or hostility, retirement from life, or slavish adherence to a particular pattern—can provide us with enough time to adjust, so long as they are not carried to excess or over long periods of time. We all go through such periods, maybe only inwardly, and all the words in the world cannot bring things back to the way they once were. In such trying times, it is not so much the actual words friends say or write as it is the simple knowledge that they are there, desiring to ease our pain, which can comfort us. Later the words will mean more.

Grief is not a state but a process, not a fixed emotional condition but a continuing movement.

Steps in Adjustment

After a time we must take steps to adjust our lives. Time, it is frequently said, is a great healer. But time alone may not be enough; we must take responsibility; the adjustment cannot be done for us. If we do not make the attempt, only more problems can result.

One of my former church members lost her husband of forty years in an automobile accident. They had been extremely close their entire married life and, having no children, had literally lived for each other. She refused to accept the fact that he was dead, would not part with any of his clothing, refused all invitations, set a place at the table for him, and even talked to him constantly. Eventually, she had to be placed in a mental institution by her distraught sisters, and she died there.

A pastor and his wife in their late fifties were shocked at the suicide of their only son, a rising young executive. The husband suffered a nervous breakdown and the wife, living with the young interim pastor and his wife, gradually developed a persecution complex, spoke incoherently, and acted irrationally. Upon learning of his wife's condition on his return to the parsonage, the husband committed suicide.

Still others dwell constantly on the topic of their grief, refusing to discuss anything or anyone else. After a time, people feel uneasy in their presence and avoid them when possible. Nothing new comes into the lives of the bereaved persons. A classic example of such constant mourning would be Queen Victoria after her consort Albert died.

Still other individuals deliberately refuse to return to the world and will themselves to die. When this death wish is paramount, doctors tell us, the patient will die, regardless of medical treatment.

Those who refuse to let go of the past, who make no attempt to cope with the problems grief has brought, who refuse help when it is offered are selfish in their mourning and can cause untold suffering for themselves and for their families and friends.

Most individuals do want to get back into the mainstream of living. They do not want to forget their grief, but neither do they want it to ruin what life remains to them. As Madame De Gasparin once wrote, "Grief is a flower as delicate and prompt to fade as happiness. Still it does not wholly die. Like the magic rose, dried and unrecognizable, a warm air breathed on it will suffice to renew its bloom." In adjusting to our grief in our personal ways we must ourselves wish to live again and make our own efforts. However, we do recognize that the grief is now part and parcel of our lives, never completely forgotten, yet not unduly dwelt upon. Clinical investigators have found that most people require from three to six months before they can actually come to terms with their loss.

Both men and women have a need to express their emotions. Sometimes we find ourselves unable to weep; our hearts are sore but our eyes remain dry. Later will come the healing power of tears, and we should welcome it. Perhaps we will shed our tears in private or in the company of close friends or family. Regardless of the place, tears shed in sincere grief do help in the process of adjustment.

A natural discussion or mention of our loss may arise. Here again we do not seek to be morbid, but if we truly believe that a person is more than the body itself, we owe it to the one we have lost not to shut him or her out of our memories or our conversation. Writing or speaking of our own particular sorrow can be a form of therapy, an aid in regaining a healthy perspective on life.

It may be necessary to make a conscious effort to turn our thoughts and actions into constructive channels. If one's child is retarded, he could actively work toward increasing aid for other children so afflicted. Such was the case with Mrs. Mary Jeffery. When her own son was born twenty-nine years ago and she learned he was retarded, she and her husband started on a small scale to give him and a few others like him homelike, residential care. Over the years this interest has grown and now Peppermint Ridge in Corona, California, is a million-dollar facility for mentally retarded children and young people who are gaining as much self-sufficiency as possible, with some achieving complete self-support. Her influence has led to the development of sheltered workshops and public school programs for the trainable mentally retarded. Out of her grief and sorrow she wrought a miracle.

If a certain illness has caused grief in the family, an active program of helping others in similar situations is a twofold blessing. It is only after one has had the experience himself that he can have true empathy with others enduring a similar difficulty.

A friend of mine, childless, recently lost her husband of thirty years. She, however, does not remain at home or satisfy herself with an occasional meeting or luncheon. Instead she keeps busy as a church deaconess, visiting new members, taking flowers to shut-ins, transporting the elderly to places they could not otherwise go. She takes care of children when their parents are facing a crisis and must be elsewhere. And above all, she radiates joy and happiness in all she does. She does not love or miss her husband any the less, but she has turned her energies and her love into worthwhile channels.

Another acquaintance has taken up courses in a local adult school, meeting new people, having interesting experiences, gaining new ideas. It has not been easy for this particular woman to take such a step; for she has always been a rather retiring individual, living for her home and family, which was broken when her husband and teen-age son were killed in a plane accident.

Still another close friend has resumed the traveling she and her husband had so enjoyed while he lived. She is still alert, going to the places they both had planned to visit, feeling closer to him because of her travel.

After a period of time has passed and efforts to resume normal living have been made, some may still find intense feelings of guilt and hostility. In such cases, professional help should be sought. While these emotions may be normal enough in the early stages of grief, if they continue and tend to submerge one's other emotions, more serious problems could arise, unless they can be objectively analyzed and dealt with.

Gradually we come to accept the fact that life does go on. And we go on—with our jobs, with our relationships to others. New doors open to new opportunities arise, changes in attitude occur. Life is dynamic, not static. No one can expect an immediate turnabout in outlook; it is gradual, but we are in no way disloyal, untrue, or selfish if we begin to live for ourselves again.

The acceptance of what cannot be changed is an inner acceptance. Just as we consciously turn toward constructive action, we must strive to accept what is past and cannot be remedied. The person with the "I must have it my way" concept or one who believes that ignoring an event will make it go away does not face reality.

In line with this acceptance is the knowledge that God has not left us; we are not alone. The person who turns from God because all is not as he wishes it to be robs himself of the opportunity to see the possibilities that lie ahead.

In the book *The Hiding Place*, Corrie Ten Boom tells of her childish fear upon seeing the corpse of a small child. Suddenly she is aware of death and fears that her beloved father will also be taken from her. She and her father are very close, and the highlights of her life as a girl are the trips on which he takes her to Amsterdam by train. In response to her anguished questioning about death, her father wisely asks if she remembers what happens each time they go through the gate which leads to the train. It is at that point that her father gives her the ticket, never before. Then he says, "And our wise father in heaven knows when we're going to need things, too. . . . When the time comes that some of us have to die, you will look into your heart and find the strength you need—just in time."[2]

Such is the faith that when grief does come to us, as come it will, God can be depended upon to give us courage, insight, strength to deal with it if we only permit him to do so. Not by chance is the 23rd Psalm frequently read at funerals or in times of great sorrow. The psalmist knew what "passing through the valley of death" meant—both for himself and for his loved ones, but his faith never faltered.

Positive Aspects

Certainly no one would ask for suffering and loss as a means to deeper understanding of others. But when grief does come our way and we pass through the various reactions and steps to readjust our lives, we find, perhaps to our astonishment, that all is not loss. There are gains, and we are better able to realize the truth of the old saying that fire is necessary to temper steel.

We find unexpected goodness in others who, while they may not be particularly articulate in expression or original in idea, do what they can to ease our sorrow. This discovery may not come to us for some time, for shock can temporarily have blocked our vision and our appreciation of others. Though the

2. Corrie Pen Boom and Elizabeth Sherrill, *The Hiding Place*, John Sherrill, ed. (Washington Depot, Conn.: Chosen Books, Inc, 1971).

ministries of friends may not be of long duration, we know and appreciate that they have reached out to us.

We find an empathy, a much more intimate emotion than mere sympathy, with others going through what we have already experienced, When my mother-in-law died after a succession of strokes over a four-year period, my wife and I had much more of a realization of the travail of a family who watches a dear one progressively waste away than we had ever had before. After our son died, we knew indeed the sorrow of other parents who had lost young children. A parent who has had a retarded child or a child afflicted with cerebral palsy, leukemia, or other debilitating disease understands the anguish of other families living through this torment and can help them, far more than can someone who has merely read articles or done studies on the subject. Is it any wonder that advances in helping these children frequently stem from both physicians and laypersons who have gone through the anguish themselves?

As a result of our own sorrow, loss, anguish, we become more useful to others. Where we once needed and received understanding, we are now in a position to reciprocate.

Our priorities change. The story is told of a father who vehemently complained of the expenses incurred in educating his daughter and who placed a price tag on the future education of his other children. But when the girl was a sophomore in college, she was killed in an automobile accident. No longer did her father have to pay for her education. He realized, too late, that his priorities had been wrong. We come to appreciate the value of life, of communication, of love, of understanding. The more material concerns no longer seem to matter. Whether or not our change in priorities stays with us or gradually fades is up to us; we have the opportunity to see what is of true value.

We come to understand that death is not the end. As the seventeenth-century poet John Donne wrote:

Death be not proud, though some have called thee
Mighty and dreadful, for thou art not so;
For those whom thou think'st thou dost overthrow
Die not, poor Death; nor yet canst thou kill me.

. . .

One short sleep past, we wake eternally;
And Death shall be no more; death, thou shalt die.

John Gunther used *Death Be Not Proud* as the title of his memorable book describing the life and death of his own young son, who in his passing defeated death and brought reassurance to his parents and friends who mourned him yet used that experience to inspire others.

There is more to life than the physical body, as the New Testament constantly tells us, and be it death, debilitating disease, or other grief, the spirit *can* conquer if we join hands with God.

Healing Helps

1. Don't be afraid to express your emotions.
2. Understand that the adjustment period will take time.
3. Seek to eliminate guilt or hostile feelings.
4. Accept in your heart that which cannot be changed.
5. Search for the positive aspects which can spring from your grief.
6. Turn to God for strength to bear whatever comes.

THE ULTIMATE HEALER

14

Prayer

Throughout this book we have been reading and thinking about thirteen sore spots which affect our lives as we go about our work, our relaxation, our relationships with others, and our moments of crisis. The suggestions given about healing these individual problems will help. There is, however, an ultimate source to which we can come for true healing, one which has been mentioned from time to time—prayer. If we believe in prayer, our lives can be enriched and made whole.

Some aspect of prayer is a part of most of our lives. For the more cynical, it is something to look on with a faint smile, as if wondering how one can be so naïve. Yet the very fact that prayer is the subject of countless books and articles, contemporary ones at that, in addition to being an integral part of various religions, indicates that prayer indeed has healing power. If only we can make use of that power which does exist and which can make our lives astonishingly new! Prayer is the response to our deepest needs.

Many individuals accept prayer as a mostly untapped source of strength and power to change mundane lives. But somehow, they feel, they are not praying in the right way and the looked-for results are elusive. If we are among these persons, we may feel encouraged by the fact that simply being *willing* to learn how to pray has put our feet on the right path.

In the learning process we must go to the right source. The poet, James Montgomery, says, "The path of prayer thyself hast trod." Christ himself is the best example of the positive results of constant prayer. He lived a life in fellowship with God at all times. The scriptures have recorded his praying at the time of his baptism, through periods of severe temptation, during the healing of the sick, before the selection of his disciples, at his Transfiguration, in the hour of danger in the garden, and with his dying breath.

Donald Culross Peattie, a distinguished naturalist and author, recalls an incident in his own early life that gave him insight about prayer. He tells of being sent across the street at the age of five to pay his tutor for a week of teaching him how to read. It was an icy, windy day, and the two-dollar bill he was clutching in his mittens blew out of his grasp. His aunt and sister, who had been watching, came out to hunt for the money but Peattie simply sat down and shut his eyes. When asked indignantly why he was not helping look for the money, he replied that he was engaged in praying they would find it.

Later in life Mr. Peattie recalled that he came to realize prayer was not some magic means by which results were brought about, simply closing the eyes and asking God to fulfill desires. It was not until Peattie became seriously ill, he said, that he truly understood the reverence of prayer which had eluded him most of his life.

There is power in prayer properly used, but this power is hammered out of or born from the iron of reality. Prayer is not a marshmallow coating spread over our daily lives so that we may attract various benefits to ourselves. Prayer is not an easy way out of a difficult situation.

The importance of private prayer cannot be overestimated.

We are all busy, and our energy and our strength are sapped by the fast pace of our living. Amidst the rush, we tend to break down, to lose direction and purpose. We will continue to be at loose ends until we accept the fact that prayer is indeed potent. If we want to accomplish, if we want to amount to something, if we want our lives to have meaning, we need to pray!

The giants of everyday life are those who have learned to pray. They too have their hardships and sufferings, to be sure, but they know that the fellowship with God in prayer can bring new strength for daily problems.

Thousands of men and women of all types and ages scoff at prayer as mere sentimentality and wishful thinking; they see themselves as "intellectuals" and "realists." Thousands more, even among the same groups, do believe in prayer in varying degrees but fear to admit such a belief lest they be laughed at by their associates. Nevertheless, we see more and more people, though unattached to any denomination or church and even tending toward skepticism and materialism, who now are seeking actively to understand the power of prayer.

Individuals who do pray are convinced that their prayers are heard and answered in some form, though rarely in dramatic events. There are times, however, when prayer truly does appear to change events in miraculous ways.

A welding inspector, trapped in an oil tank on a ship, prayed that someone would hear his cries before he smothered and open the tank cover, securely fastened from the outside. Then, in the darkness, this man decided he could not tell God how to act. He must await the Lord's reply to his need. Meanwhile, in the tomblike atmosphere, his hands reached out, seemingly guided to the proper bolts to turn. At last he was able to loosen the cover and push it back. Above him were the stars.

Dr. C. Everett Koop, who in Philadelphia in 1974 successfully separated a rare set of Siamese twins, claims a "complete belief in the sovereignty of God." Chief surgeon of the University of Pennsylvania Children's Hospital and one of the world's leading pediatric surgeons, Dr. Koop, along with the hospital and medical team, donated the services that separated the children of a poor family in the Dominican Republic. "My surgical skills are a gift from God. Thank God for them," Dr. Koop tells grateful families. He believes that God is in control of all circumstances and events and that "knowing that someone else is running the show gives me a tremendous amount of comfort." Prior to the unusual surgery on the twins, Koop asked for the prayers of the Medical Assistance Programs, Inc., staff on behalf of the relatively rare operation.

Answers to prayer come in a multitude of ways that cannot be anticipated. In most instances there are no thunderbolts from heaven but rather an orderly unfolding whereby things work out. Regardless of the way, regardless of the answer, prayer is heard. We may have doubts. Perhaps God does not respond as quickly as we would prefer; perhaps we are not willing to accept the answer when it does come.

Some years ago, a member of my church gave me a copy of a poem by Eliza Hickok on prayer. She said its contents had often helped her in moments of doubt.

> I know not by what methods rare,
> But this I know, God answers prayer.
> I know not when he sends the word
> That tells us fervent prayer is heard;
> I know it cometh, soon or late,
> Therefore we need to pray and wait.

> I know not if the blessings sought
> Will come in just the guise I thought.
> I leave my prayer to him alone
> Whose will is wiser than my own.[1]

Prayer is communication with God, but we cannot manipulate God through means of prayer. It cannot be simply a request for whatever we desire, however worthy this desire appears to us. To view prayer in such a shallow way is to invite disillusionment and cynicism. The farmer who prays for rain for his corn cannot feel his desires have not been heard if the rain does not fall as he requests. Prayer is an act of trust that the Creator has the power to change things, but it also is an act of humility and submission of our will to his.

We may still petition God for his personal favor in moments of emergency and peril. Prayers have an added power when, in our very helplessness, we commit ourselves completely to God's power and goodness rather than insist we alone are masters of our fate.

A story is told of a British regiment in which every man carried a copy of the 91st Psalm with him and read it every day. A portion of that psalm contains the words:

> He who dwells in the shelter of the Most High,
> who abides in the shadow of the Almighty,
> will say to the Lord, "My refuge and my fortress;
> my God in whom I trust." (Ps. 91: 1,2)

It is said that in four years of frontline warfare, this particular regiment did not suffer a single casualty. Coincidence? A miracle? An answer to daily prayer in the words of the

1. Eliza M. Hickok, "God Answers Prayer" from *The Best Loved Religious Poems*, James G. Lawson, comp. (Old Tappan, N.J.: Fleming H. Revell, 1933).

psalmist? Yet were there not other regiments whose men also prayed just as fervently but who suffered casualties? Prayers are lifted, petitions are heard, yet we cannot presume to dictate the answers by means of our all too human, fallible reasoning.

Prayer touches a force open to us all, those of us willing to learn and practice the selfless love that is required. The mechanics, the modus operandi of effective prayer are complex and difficult to understand. We do not know why some prayers appear to have an affirmative answer and others, equally worthy in our eyes, receive what we see as a negative response or, worse still, none at all. Why, for example, do sincere prayers for the starving of drought-stricken nations seem unavailing? Why are innocent persons the victims of crime and disease? This is the heart of the great mystery of prayer. Why, indeed, should we pray at all?

Prayer Helps Us Cope

Wernher von Braun, director of the NASA Space Center, once said in an interview, in discussing his personal prayer life:

> Shortly after the end of World War II, I came to understand that religion is not a cathedral inherited from the past, not a quick prayer at the last minute. To be effective, religion has to be backed up by discipline and effort. Gradually I came to feel that in order to be realistic, my prayers too needed to move into a new dimension. I began to pray daily, hourly, instead of on occasion. I took long rides into the desert where I could be alone with my prayer. I prayed with my wife in the evening. As I tried to understand my problems, I tried to find God's will in acting on them. In this age of space

flight and nuclear fission, to use power wisely calls for moral and ethical climate. We can achieve it only through many hours of the deep concentration we call prayer.

A doctor of my acquaintance the night before surgery goes to his patient's room and has a word of prayer with him. This surgeon has found that in the daily routine of living, conversing with God brings astonishing benefits. It has the power to help him cope with whatever his situation might be, and, of course, it has a healing power for his patient.

The Apollo 13 astronauts in a television broadcast described their harrowing return from outer space after an explosion ripped their spacecraft as it sped toward the moon. The 87-hour struggle riveted the attention of the world on their plight. John Swigert said their safe return was an answer to prayer.

"If you are asking me whether I prayed, I certainly did," he told the listening world at a dinner in New York following his return from space. "And I have no doubt that perhaps my prayers and the prayers of the rest of the people did an awful lot, contributed an awful lot for us getting back."

Prayer makes possible the inner transformation of the one who prays as well as the one who is prayed for. God acts on the inner man to bring about a relaxed receptivity, empowering him to move from task to task with serenity rather than with anxiety and frustration. Upsetting trivialities are pushed aside and he can find his way again.

Although there is no set of infallible directions for prayer, we certainly can follow some steps in order to understand and get the most out of this communication with God.

Practical Prayer Power

If we are sincere in our desire to learn to pray, we must be willing to look seriously at the steps in the learning process.

Even the disciples, who were close to Jesus, felt impelled to ask him to teach them to pray. We too seek guidance.

1. *Motive*. Perspective is important. Looking from the Jersey bank over the Hudson River toward Manhattan, one can see the twin towers of the World Trade Center rising majestically heavenward. Yet other buildings are just as important. The whole skyline must be seen in perspective. In the same way, prayer sets the perspective for our relationships with our neighbors and the world. It is a means for self-understanding which can lead to self-realization, not wrought by self but by God. Prayer is what we do so that God can do something with us and to us; it is preparing the way for God. We make ourselves open to God through prayer so that he can enter our lives and transform us.

Self-understanding does not come easily, and prayer helps us get rid of some of our myopic illusions. The right motive for prayer starts us on the path toward overcoming self-deception. Hate, anger, despondency, fear, despair, pride, envy—all can be drawn into the open, and we can see ourselves as we really are.

2. *Place*. It has become a cliché to say that man can pray anywhere. Admittedly, too many of us tend to confine our prayer moments to a specific building or room. The point is not so much that we *can* pray anywhere but rather *do* we? The effectiveness of our prayers in exceptional circumstances usually depends on the steadiness with which we have prayed daily in quiet places, free from noise and other distractions. The place of prayer was important to our Lord; is it any less so to us? When he wanted to pray, he frequently went apart—to a mountain, to a garden, to a quiet room.

Free from outside distractions, we can give God the opportunity to speak to us. We can slow down and work toward an inner peace. There is great value in praying habitually in one place, in entering the "spiritual closet" and shutting the door to outside diversions.

An old French peasant made frequent trips to the village

church and spent long periods within. He sat or knelt in the back pew in complete silence. One day someone who had often seen the old man come and go went into the church and, finding him in his pew, asked, "What are you doing here all alone? Why do you come so often?" The old man replied simply, "I am looking at God and God is looking at me." When we withdraw from the frantic cycle of work and the rush of duties, we can get a better look at God and he at us.

Private places of prayer vary. Some individuals like to pray by a window, looking out at the beauty and order of the world of nature. Others pray by their bedsides, feeling rest and strength come to them there. Others sit in a corner of a room with devotional books close at hand, finding the help and wisdom of others as a source of their own prayer. Still others feel a closeness to God when looking through books which include pictures, poetry, and quotations.

3. *Time.* We can, of course, pray at any hour of the day or night. Some persons pray more frequently than others. However, it is helpful to discipline one's self to a certain time of day. The body likes regularity; so does the spirit.

Morning and evening are the two periods of the day which best lend themselves to prayer. Morning is effective, for then one is rested and restored physically. That is, unless one has had a particularly wild time the evening before and awakens with a throbbing headache. At such a time, perhaps, the one-sentence prayer, "Lord, help me never to get in such a mess again!" might be the only prayer that comes to mind. But under normal circumstances, morning is a good time to breathe a prayer. Quiet music may help set the proper mood. For example, a friend of mine wore out several recordings that included a choir of monks chanting the Easter Gregorian chant, using the record consistently to aid in his morning devotions.

With the availability of cassette tape recorders, it is possible to tape one's own early-morning mood music. The singing of the church choir, concert music, or contemporary songs are only a few of the limitless possibilities to be recorded.

Morning prayer can set our bearings so that we are able to face whatever the day may bring—an unpleasant confrontation, a tense situation, a problem which we must solve. To ask for help and to expect that help are sure steps in the right direction. Surely such benefits are worth rising half an hour earlier than usual.

The evening hour probably affords us the most convenient opportunity to pray. Unfortunately, our minds, by that time, have become so cluttered with work we have brought home, with television programs, and with problems of the day that setting aside a quiet moment for prayer in the evening requires real effort.

In earlier times, there was little to do after work in the evening and before time for bed but take down the family Bible, read, and pray, many times as a family. In this context, I remember my own mother sitting at the foot of the bed, reading to my sister and me from the Scriptures. I now realize how much the experience influenced my outlook on life.

Today, however, our evening hours are taken up with a myriad of activities, and our subconscious minds are concerned with these thoughts rather than spiritual ones. We would benefit if, instead, we set aside a portion of time before sleep for thoughts of gratitude and intercession, an opportunity to open our minds to God. We might conclude such thoughts with, "Give me this night a quiet mind. Free me from anxiety. Let me awaken refreshed and ready for new tasks tomorrow." Such quiet reflections can help avoid repetition of past mistakes. The Hebrew psalmist wrote, "My mouth praises you with joyful lips when I think of thee upon my bed, and meditate on thee in the watches of the night; for thou hast been my help, and in the shadow of thy wings I sing for joy." (Ps. 63: 5-7)

Morning and evening are the traditional prayer times. That

does not mean, however, that we are to shut our minds to prayer at other times of the day. Circumstances not only alter cases but also determine when prayer can be most effective for the individual. Conversation with God can be held at any time, even while one is busy with mundane responsibilities. Pray *when* you feel like it, *where* you feel like it, and *as* you feel like it.

Deal with problems or joys prayerfully as you encounter them, sharing them quickly and quietly.

4. *Position.* Actually, there is no one best position for prayer except as you, the individual, choose. Followers of transcendental meditation may sit motionless for long periods of time, turning their thoughts inward so as to become more spiritually aware. Devotees of yoga may assume the lotus position for purposes of prayerful thought. Some may even feel that standing for lengthy periods on one's head can clarify thoughts. Some persons find they pray best when kneeling and closing their eyes. Others take long walks alone. Still others sit quietly in a place apart from distraction.

The position for prayer depends entirely on the person involved. If one has had a prayerful experience in a particular spot or position, he may tend to return to it. A great deal is a result of one's training, or lack of training, in the past where prayer is concerned. The main thing is that one *does* pray, coming into communication with God, listening for his answers, waiting for his peace. Faith and belief are essential to enter into the spirit of prayer; skepticism can be a stumbling block.

5. *The heart.* We hear a great deal about the heart these days. We are alert to the many things that can go wrong with this vital organ. The ancients believed the emotions were centered in the heart, and there has been a carry-over of this idea in contemporary expressions such as "heart's desire," "home is where the heart is," "heartfelt thanks." We hear, "Let us open our hearts to God."

Svetlana Alliluyeva Stalin, the daughter of the deceased dictator of the Soviet Union, came to the United States and rejected the beliefs for which her father had stood. She wrote in one of her books that religion had done much to change her. "I was brought up in a family where there was never any talk of God. But when I became a grown person, I found that it was impossible to exist without God in one's heart."[2]

The lifeblood of prayer is seated in the heart, in the emotions. An open heart means letting God work his will. Words are frequently less important in prayer than silence; if we pray by speaking, we pray more significantly by listening. We are to "wait upon the Lord" in our prayers; we are to wait quietly, patiently, and expectantly with our emotions as well as with our minds.

Try This

No one but you yourself can cultivate your prayer life. Prayer cultivation takes both discipline and effort. False, negative thoughts can sear and weaken prayer, while positive, affirmative thoughts can heal and strengthen. You may wish to adapt some of the following suggestions to your personality and to your individual needs.

1. On awakening, make a positive affirmation. Let yourself go and share with God what is on your mind. "This is the day which the Lord has made. I will be glad and rejoice."

2. While dressing or going to work, whistle or sing a hymn or song that means a lot to you. Personally, I whistle when I get off the elevator in the building where I work, but I would sing if I could carry a tune.

3. Think about God during the day. In faces, in the printed word, in photographs, in the world about you—see if you can

2. Svetlana Alliluyeva Stalin, *Twenty Letters to a Friend* (New York: Harper & Row, 1963).

see God. Thank him for opportunities and share your concerns with him. Live on a mountaintop metaphorically and look up to see the stars; climb even if you occasionally slip into the valley.

4. See in each responsibility more than merely a chore to be completed as expeditiously as possible. Look at your task as containing a purpose, an opportunity.

5. Have confidence that God is helping you. Operate under the assumption that you cannot change others and accept the concept that you can change only yourself. Then do it.

6. At some time during the day, relax your mind and body—condition your consciousness.

7. As you arise and before you go to bed, take a few moments for quiet meditation.

8. Make your last waking thought one of committal to God.

Following these disciplines conscientiously will result in God's healing your life.